ADVANCE PRAISE

"This is far more than a banking story. Ralph shows what bold, customer-centric leadership looks like in an industry under immense pressure. His candor about the wins, setbacks, and reca-librations makes this book invaluable for any executive leading large-scale change."

—Jamie Dimon, Chairman and CEO of JPMorganChase

"The shift Ralph describes—moving from products to customer experience—reshaped ING from the inside out. If you want to understand how ING became the leading digital primary bank, read this. It is one of the clearest articulations of customer-centric strategy I've come across."

—Ajay Banga, former CEO of Mastercard

"Ralph's visionary leadership and the successful transformation of ING to a leader in digital banking has been an inspiration for many other CEOs in the financial industry and beyond. He set the bar—and did it early before it was popular and clear that it needed to be done. And the legacy stands."

—Dominic Barton, Chairman of Rio Tinto, former Global Managing Partner at McKinsey, and former Ambassador of Canada to China

"Ralph's success is about leading with purpose and sticking to consistency. His book shows that staying true to your purpose is key to any successful business transformation. I was especially taken aback by his drive to lead the sustainability efforts in global banking."

—Jan Peter Balkenende, Minister of State and former Prime Minister of the Netherlands, Professor Emeritus at Erasmus University Rotterdam, and Senior Advisor to EY and FGS Global

"You don't need to be in financial services to learn from this book. Ralph's framework for clarity, alignment, simplification, and agile execution applies to any complex organization facing disruption. Today, disruptions from geopolitics, technology, and trade plus the AI revolution require every CEO to guide their organization through unprecedented uncertainty, make hard calls, and keep stakeholders aligned through continuous change. His experience in transforming ING is a must-read for leaders in how to deal with disruption."

—Axel Weber, Chairman of Raisin, former President of Deutsche Bundesbank, and former Chairman of UBS Group

"ING's early digital transformation generates valuable insights as to the importance of the personal drive of a CEO. It shows the importance for CEOs to stick to long-term vision while being open to short-term adaptation when dealing with an ever-changing context."

—Hans Wijers, former Minister of Economic Affairs for the Netherlands, former CEO of Akzo Nobel, and former Chairman of ING

"Ralph gives us the clearest blueprint I've seen for what any company dealing with AI must do to survive the next decade: simplify relentlessly, align around purpose, and innovate faster than the market. This book should be required reading for every CEO."

—David Bach, President of IMD Business School and Nestlé Professor of Strategy

DO YOUR THING

LESSONS FROM BANKING'S
BIGGEST DIGITAL TRANSFORMATION

DO YOUR THING

RALPH HAMERS

Former CEO of ING and UBS

COPYRIGHT © 2026 RALPH HAMERS
All rights reserved.

DO YOUR THING
Lessons from Banking's Biggest Digital Transformation

FIRST EDITION

ISBN   978-1-5445-5203-3 *Hardcover*
          978-1-5445-5202-6 *Paperback*
          978-1-5445-5204-0 *Ebook*

ralphhamers.com

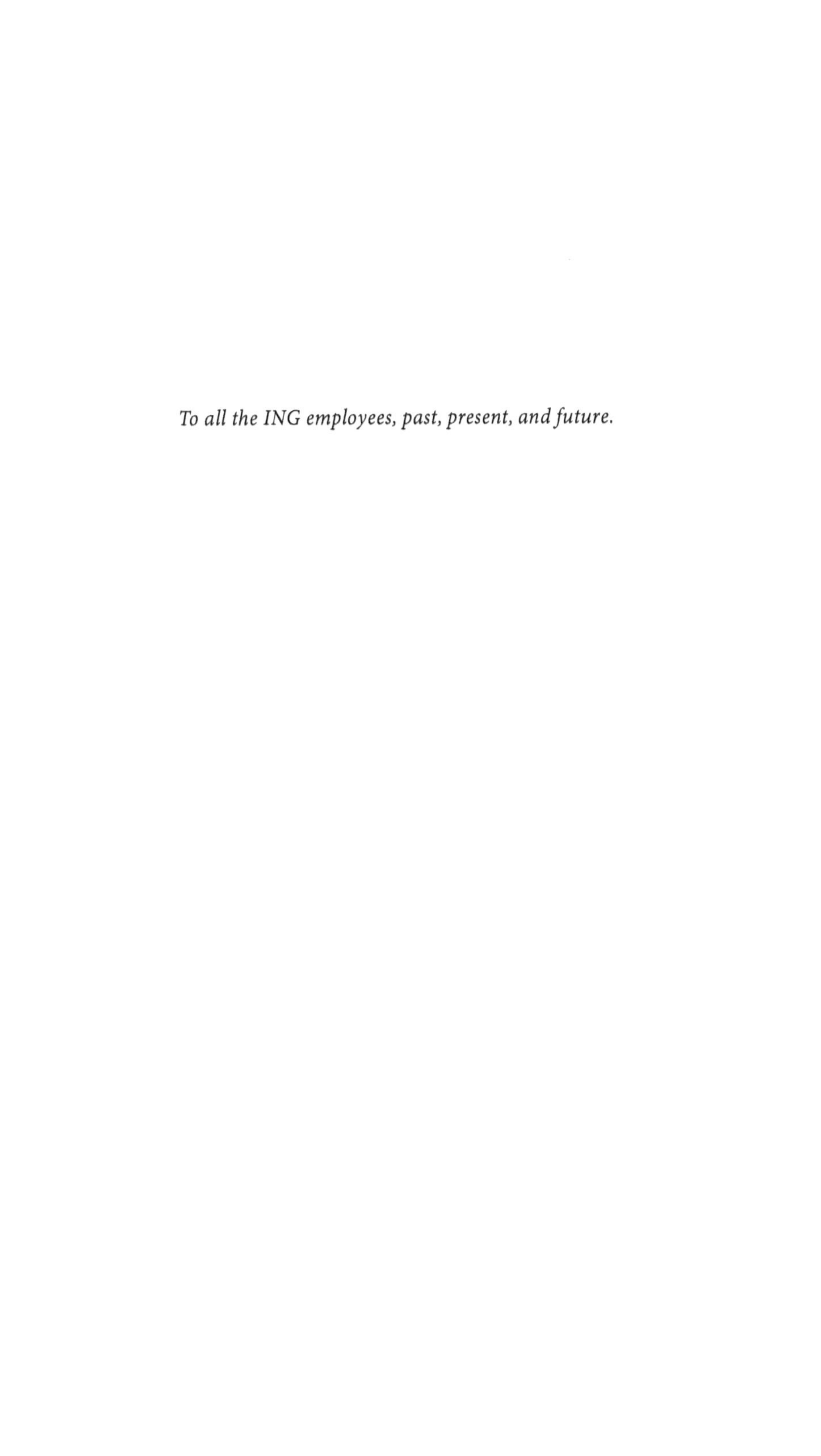

To all the ING employees, past, present, and future.

CONTENTS

FOREWORD 11

INTRODUCTION 21

1. ING IN NEED OF TRANSFORMATION 29
2. THE SUN RISES ORANGE 43
3. THE POWER OF PURPOSE 79
4. LEADING THE TRANSFORMATION 91
5. CUSTOMER AT THE CORE 131
6. THE BLUEPRINT OF A DIGITAL BANK 155
7. THE NEW WAY OF WORKING 185
8. ING'S CAMPUS 207
9. LIVING THE BRAND 223
10. IMPACT AT SCALE 255
11. THE NEXT FRONTIER 279

CONCLUSION 301

ACKNOWLEDGMENTS 309

ABOUT THE AUTHOR 313

NOTES 317

FOREWORD

—Jeroen van der Veer, former Chairman
of the Supervisory Board, ING Group;
former CEO, Royal Dutch Shell

When I first joined the Supervisory Board of ING in the midst of the financial crisis, I entered an organization facing extraordinary pressure on all fronts. The global banking system was shaken. Public trust had evaporated. Regulatory institutions were demanding more capital at the very moment capital was hardest to find. Europe was tightening constraints on banks that had already weathered years of instability. At ING, we were contending simultaneously with capital shortages, state aid repayment requirements, and a forced divestment of our insurance businesses, each with compressed timelines and significant financial consequences. It was, in every sense, a perfect storm.

Yet what struck me then, and remains vivid today, was not only the scale of the external challenges but the internal ones: how to maintain motivation in an organization burdened by restructurings, reductions, and public scrutiny. Employees were working tirelessly to keep the bank stable, even as they faced uncertainty about their future. In such moments, leadership is not simply about solving technical problems; it is about restoring direction, discipline, and belief. As chairman, I carried the responsibility of helping steer ING through one of the most consequential periods in its history.

It was against this backdrop that we set out to select a new CEO, someone who would not only guide ING out of the crisis but position it for the future. The profile we created was clear: the bank needed a leader with passion for a new strategic direction, the speed and conviction to drive it, and the courage to make difficult decisions with clarity and purpose. We were not looking merely for a caretaker. We were looking for a catalyst.

The selection process itself was unconventional by industry standards, and perhaps even by common sense. We conducted competitive interviews at a surprise board meeting. Candidates were given just two questions and 40 minutes to prepare:

1. If you were appointed CEO today, what would be your strategy?
2. Given that strategy, what changes would you make to the top team?

No pre-reading, no strategic decks, no rehearsed narratives. Just clarity of thought under pressure. In that environment, one designed to surface genuine capability, not polished performance, Ralph Hamers distinguished himself immediately. His answers were not only compelling; they reflected a deep understanding of where banking was heading and how quickly ING would need to move. Ralph came out of that process as the clear choice.

Selecting him was not without risk. Ralph was young relative to predecessors. He was leading ING Belgium, one of the large business units, but was not on the executive board. He was chosen over several executive board members who had expected to be considered "next in line." Ralph effectively "jumped over" the entire executive layer, something I had never seen done successfully at a major global bank. The Supervisory Board felt strongly: the future belonged to leaders who understood the digital shift, who could energize an organization, and who had the ambition to move decisively rather than incrementally. Ralph was that leader.

There was no nervousness on my part once he began. As a nonexecutive chairman, my role was not to run the bank but to ensure its leadership could. In those early months, Ralph and I spoke frequently. He was never afraid to raise challenges, to ask for perspective, or to confront realities directly. Those conversations, often on Sunday evenings or early Monday mornings, demonstrated responsibility. A leader who names problems early is a leader who solves them before they become crises.

What Ralph brought to ING was more than a strategy. He brought perspective, a new horizon for a bank that had spent years defending, repairing, and navigating constraints. His vision of a fully digital, streamlined, and customer-centric bank resonated deeply across the organization. Although it had sold its digital banking activities in the US and Canada, ING still had strong digital foundations in places like Germany, Spain, France, Italy, and Australia; Ralph saw that potential and accelerated it dramatically. For employees exhausted by crisis management, this shift was energizing. Suddenly, they were not simply trying to survive; they were building the future. Employee commitment rose quickly under his leadership, precisely because a compelling strategy can be one of the most powerful sources of motivation.

Ralph understood something essential: that speed matters. Banking was changing faster than many expected, and ING's future advantage would depend on its ability to act while others hesitated. His approach was not reckless: it was disciplined, structured, and aligned with a long-term vision.

It was determined, and that made all the difference.

The transformation that followed—ING's shift toward a digital-first operating model, the reorganization of leadership structures, the introduction of agile ways of working, and the creation of a unified global platform—required boldness, resilience, and a willingness to challenge convention. Ralph led with all three.

As chairman during those years, I had the privilege of watching him grow into the role, drive a clear strategic agenda, and reinvigorate the organization. ING emerged from the crisis not only stronger but *ahead* of the industry, a testament to leadership that is both visionary and practical.

This book tells the story of that transformation from Ralph's perspective, but as someone who observed it closely, I can say this: ING's success in those years was no accident. It was the product of clarity in crisis, conviction in strategy, and courage in execution. Ralph Hamers embodied it all.

It is my pleasure to introduce this narrative and the lessons within it. For leaders navigating uncertainty, for organizations seeking renewal, and for anyone interested in how a century-old institution can reinvent itself for the digital age, Ralph's story offers not only insight but inspiration.

A few thoughts

Some people in our society feel threatened
Others are optimistic
Still others feel cheated
We're opening borders
And closing them down
Getting richer
And getting poorer
Worry has infected investor confidence
And assumptions of endless growth
Eroded by fears of decline

It's quite a time to be alive
Not long ago, things were different
Times were great
Borrowing was seen as a right
No capital? No problem.
New markets
A new economy
Caution was ridiculed

And at the coronation of growth
Greed snuck in disguised as optimism
When the hurricane hit
We found ourselves at the epicenter
And were humbled
That mistakes were made is now well understood
But we have fought back
Faced down adversity
And we are still here

The time has come to remind ourselves
Of who we are
Where do we want to be?

Ten years ago, Twitter was a bird sound
Cloud was in the sky
4G was a parking space
And Google a sound
This may be a time of rapid change
But the truth is
The pace of change will never be slower than it is today
Our past innovations are no entitlement to a future

Customers imagine new services before we develop them
Banks may not survive
But banking will

This is a race for the energetic
For the competitive
For those who can deploy strength
With velocity
To deliver better value to those we serve
For it is our customers who decide our success
And while they are central to all we do
We accept that mostly they're not thinking of us
At all
They are busy
With this
And this
Getting on with their lives
With confidence
A belief in hard work
And a faith in simple dreams

We are not here to change them
We are here to salute them
To tell them: You can do it!
In a fast-moving age
Where the next move is not always obvious
We are here to help them forward
To make new steps
Important steps
Joyful steps
Ambitious steps
Forward looking steps
In every walk of life
From here
To here

Empowering people
To stay a step ahead
In life and in business

(Think Forward)[1]

INTRODUCTION

Many business leaders underestimate what real transformation requires. The biggest problem isn't that they completely lack strategy or long-term vision; they can always hire consultants to help them be bold or communications experts to help them craft their message. Many underestimate how long true transformation takes, how disciplined the leadership must be, and how much consistency is required to sustain it.

Too often, leaders fall into the trap of believing transformation is a linear plan to be executed, when it's a long, *non*linear journey that demands both zooming out on direction and zooming *in* on short-term progress. They either default to command-and-control, which kills empowerment and agility, or they empower without structure, which breeds chaos. Real transformation requires balancing both styles: enough control to ensure focus and enough empowerment to unlock change. That's what keeps everyone aligned while allowing innovation and ownership to thrive.

However, many leaders never get started because they're afraid to make a mistake. They wait for the perfect plan before acting, forgetting that execution will be *im*perfect anyway. In most areas (outside of strict regulatory or legal obligations) 80 percent is good enough. Moving fast and learning along the way beats waiting for flawless design.

By embracing the 80 percent solution, they can make faster, more confident decisions and create a culture that learns and adapts, rather than hesitates in pursuit of perfection, while leading their transformation with clarity and consistency.

AI THE DISRUPTER

What makes this story relevant today is not nostalgia. It's timing.

This is the story of how ING transformed into a digital bank the moment digitalization began to disrupt banking fundamentally. At the time, digital was not an add-on or an efficiency play; it was reshaping customer expectations, business models, and the role of banks in society. We didn't know exactly where it would lead, but we knew that standing still was not an option.

Today, leaders across every industry are facing a similar moment, only faster and more intense. Artificial intelligence is disrupting how organizations operate, decide, and compete. Like digital once did for banking, AI is forcing leaders to rethink what their organizations are for, how value is created, and what kind of leadership is required when change accelerates faster than certainty.

That is why this book matters now. Not because ING's transformation was perfect, and not because our journey can be copied, but because the patterns are familiar. The same questions are resurfacing:

- How deeply do we transform?
- How fast do we move?

- How do we keep people aligned when the ground keeps shifting beneath us?

The answers we discovered then about purpose, customers, and brand are even more critical in the age of AI.

LEADERS FACING TRANSFORMATION

This book is for business leaders, especially CEOs and executives, who are facing transformation. These are people responsible for steering large organizations through change, often after years of half-hearted or underestimated transformation efforts. They've seen initiatives come and go but few that truly reshape culture, align strategy, and deliver lasting results.

It's for leaders who want to understand not just what ING did but how it was done and how those lessons can apply to their own organizations. Some may naturally be bold communicators or visionary strategists; others may rely on teams or consultants to help them build those skills. Either way, this book shows that what truly matters isn't charisma or vision alone; it's consistency.

These leaders want to know how to keep their people aligned, balance empowerment with structure, and lead through long, nonlinear journeys of change. They're not looking for abstract theory or academic models. They're looking for a framework grounded in real experience...one that connects purpose, culture, brand, leadership, and execution into a single, actionable system.

This book is for leaders who are ready to transform their organizations and themselves.

A STORY AND A FRAMEWORK

The story is not about my seven years at ING, the financial or regulatory developments in those years, ING's financial or commercial success, or every eventful moment. This book is about transformation. Its purpose is to share learning and to inspire leaders to approach comprehensive transformation if they see the need for it.

Leaders can expect two things from this book: a story and a framework.

I've been asked by business leaders and consultants to explain what made ING's transformation successful: what we did right, what we got wrong, and how we managed to move an entire organization in one direction. I've told this story many times, but writing this book allows me to share the full picture:

- How transformation really happens
- What it demands of leaders
- What consistency looks like in practice

The story is how ING transformed from a financial conglomerate in need of government help during the financial crisis into one that became the *Global Finance Best Bank in the World*. It's the story of how 54,000 people aligned behind a shared purpose, rebuilt their confidence, and learned to act as one. It's an honest account of what worked, what didn't, and what we learned along the way.

It's also a book about learning through imperfection. Leaders will read stories of where we succeeded but also of where we failed or had to adjust.

No leader gets everything right. If you dare to experiment, you will fall sometimes, but it's about getting up and how you move forward.

Transformation doesn't follow a straight line, and neither did ours. Sometimes you'll have to adapt to short-term issues.

The framework is what ties it all together. It's the structure we used (sometimes consciously, sometimes intuitively) to make sure every part of the organization moved in sync. It connects purpose externally to strategy, customer promise, and brand and internally to leadership, culture (behavior), and execution:

- Purpose
- Strategy
- Customer promise
- Brand and reputation
- Leadership, talent, and capabilities
- Culture and behavior
- Incentives
- Execution

Leaders will see how these pieces fit together, how they (and only they) must connect the dots, and how this consistency across them creates momentum and builds trust.

They'll see real transformation sustained over time, too. This book helps leaders close the gap between ambition and execution. It teaches them how to think holistically, act decisively, and stay consistent so transformation isn't a slogan but a sustained way of leading.

NOT A UNIVERSAL ANSWER

The framework itself emerged from experience: what we learned leading ING's transformation and from the mistakes we made along the way. Readers can use it as a guide, take what fits, and adapt it to their own context. I don't claim to have the universal answer; I'm simply showing what worked for us and why.

What this book is not is a management theory or an academic study. I'm not a guru, and I haven't analyzed hundreds of other leaders to extract a formula for success. This isn't about buzzwords or corporate slogans; it's about how to lead real people through real change.

It's also not a step-by-step manual promising that if you copy what we did, you'll get the same results. Every company is different, and every leader has to find their own way. What is offered here is a way of thinking that you can adapt to your own context. You can take five of my ideas, combine them with yours, and make it work.

Transformation doesn't come from one brilliant moment or a single big decision. It comes from connecting the dots and managing them every day, with intention, discipline, and conviction.

TRANSFORMATION IS NEVER PERFECT

I've lived what I'm describing. Over seven years, together with 54,000 colleagues, we transformed ING from a bank that needed government help after the financial crisis into one that was recognized as the best bank in the world. That journey wasn't perfect, far from it, but it was real, and it worked.

There's also a personal reason. I'm proud of what we achieved at ING. We rose from the ashes of the financial crisis and rebuilt not just a business but a culture: a company with purpose, pride, and confidence. This book is a way to honor the people who made that possible. The ones who have "orange blood" running through their veins, as we say at ING. It is as much for them as it is for leaders facing transformation.

My deeper purpose is to help other leaders succeed in their own transformations. Too many organizations get stuck in the same patterns: bold ambitions, half-hearted plans, inconsistent execution, and short-termism, the idea of giving up when the going gets tough instead of pushing through the "valley of despair" when you feel like you aren't making progress. I want to show that transformation isn't magic. It's a mindset and a method. It can't be delegated, but it can be learned.

I've made mistakes, and I want to help others avoid them. I hope this book gives leaders the confidence to start, the structure to stay consistent, and the clarity to finish.

If it helps even a few move their organizations forward with greater purpose and discipline, then it will have fulfilled its purpose, and so will I.

A successful transformation is never perfect, because it's in the mistakes where the learning happens. Transformation is about daring to try, adjusting fast, and moving forward.

I hope this book is engaging to read. It's a story about people, leadership, and change told from experience, not theory. By the end, leaders will not only understand what ING did, but they'll have the tools and mindset to lead their own transformation with purpose, clarity, and consistency.

Transformation is easy to describe in hindsight. Living through it is something else entirely. To understand why our journey unfolded the way it did, you have to go back to where ING stood before we began.

ING IN NEED OF TRANSFORMATION

ING's transformation was not born out of the financial crisis alone. The crisis forced us to restructure, but the real imperative was digitalization. While we were fighting to survive, technology was reshaping banking at a pace that made our existing model unsustainable; it was literally a perfect storm that removed any room for delay.

In 2006, ING was on top of the world. The flagship brand was very well recognized globally; ING Direct was well-known in Australia, Canada, and the US.

It was one of the top ten financial services companies, overall being number two in revenue, number nine in market cap, and number four in brand value in the world.

In 2008, few inside ING Group could have predicted just how deeply the global financial crisis would shake the institution. Like many others, ING had exposure to mortgage-backed securities (Alt-A) that were thought to be safe. When the markets collapsed, ING needed government support, twice. Confidence was rattled, both internally and externally. The CEO and CFO stepped down.

The European Commission (EC) imposed a significant restructuring in the aftermath. Jan Hommen stepped in as CEO to steady the ship. He moved quickly and, at times, ruthlessly to restore order and reposition the company toward banking. It was a difficult period, marked by uncertainty and loss but also by the beginning of something new.

Jan's leadership laid the groundwork for ING's later transformation. By the time I stepped in, ING had been through crisis and restructuring. What people needed most was hope and a vision for the future.

TWO GOVERNMENT RESCUES

During the height of the global financial crisis, ING Group received a €10 billion capital injection from the Dutch government. On October 19, the Dutch State announced the rescue as part of a broader €20 billion support package aimed at stabilizing fundamentally healthy financial institutions. A few weeks later, the transaction was finalized, with the State acquiring nonvoting, core Tier 1 securities in ING, receiving an annual interest of 8.5 percent and the right to nominate two members to ING's Supervisory Board.

The capital injection raised ING's Tier 1 capital ratio from 6.5 percent to around 8 percent, providing a much-needed buffer against further financial instability. As part of the agreement, ING suspended dividend payments, and thousands of people lost their jobs.

To further reduce risk, ING entered an Illiquid Assets

Back-Up Facility (IABF) with the Dutch government. On January 26, 2009, ING transferred 80 percent of the economic interest in a €30 billion portfolio of US Alt-A mortgage-backed securities to the State. This move significantly lowered ING's exposure to illiquid, high-risk assets and helped restore market confidence.

Michel Tilmant stepped down as CEO of ING Group on January 26, 2009, citing "extraordinary developments over the past few months" and his personal condition. He remained with the company as an advisor until his retirement on August 1, 2009.

Following his resignation, Eric Boyer de la Giroday, a member of the Executive Board since 2004, served as acting CEO. Jan Hommen, then chairman of ING's Supervisory Board, was nominated to become the new CEO, pending approval at the General Meeting of Shareholders on April 27, 2009.

THE COST OF PUBLIC OWNERSHIP

Once state support is involved, politics begins to feel ownership of the company being supported. They believe they have a say. Bonuses and executive pay are immediately questioned.

When ING received state support, everything changed. Restructuring wasn't optional; it was mandated. For many leaders, it felt like tearing down something they had spent decades building. The emotional weight of that was real.

At the same time, becoming a state-supported bank meant stepping into a harsh spotlight. Suddenly, everyone had an opinion: politicians, the press, the public. Banks were held responsible for everything that went wrong, and the criticism was relentless. Inside the organization, people had to adapt not only to new rules but to a new reality: one shaped by scrutiny and skepticism, which required behavioral change and the slow rebuilding of trust while having to adapt to massive adjustments within the organization.

Being a banker became something to hide. People avoided social events just to avoid admitting where they worked.

THE EMOTIONAL TOLL

There was an emotional weight behind all of this that few people saw. The facts were in the headlines, but the internal experience was different.

There was fear and denial because ING's equity was hit. Everyone watched the market value of its assets fall and capital ratios suffer.

But experience told a different story. The underlying mortgages weren't as bad as the panic suggested, but financial markets don't wait for the truth. They overreact with optimism *and* with fear. In 2008, fear took over: the financial world was terrified by the scale of the US mortgage crisis.

The whole experience was humbling and frightening. ING people were working night and day fighting to save the company, to right its wrongs.

They still cared about doing the right thing.

JAN HOMMEN STEPS IN

Jan Hommen was a well-known name in the Netherlands. He had been CFO at Philips and, before that, at Alcoa, a US-based mining company. He had also served on the Supervisory Board of Ahold Delhaize and was chairman of the Supervisory Board at ING before he stepped in as CEO. He had serious corporate experience and a strong restructuring track record.

Jan wasn't a banker, but he was meticulous and tough. He was the guy who could cut costs, make hard decisions, and get things done. That's what ING needed, and he made it his mission to get the company out of restructuring as quickly as possible, because the political hostility toward banks was intense.

Jan brought with him decades of leadership experience; he understood how to stabilize a company, and that background was invaluable. More importantly, he wanted to help. He didn't come in to play the hero; he came in to clean up the mess.

ING had two primary goals. First, it needed to raise capital, because banks were widely seen as undercapitalized heading into the crisis. Second, it had to repay the Dutch government.

It wasn't as simple as "Repay the government and you're done." No. ING needed to repay the government *and* strengthen its capital base.

ING was under a strict performance timeline. If it didn't meet the targets, the EC would impose even more restructuring measures.

Jan executed through divestments and vigorous cost-cutting, doing everything necessary to keep the company alive and get it healthy again.

On April 9, 2009, the "Back to Basics" program was launched.

ING will reduce its geographic and business scope. Smaller businesses with no clear outlook for market leadership consume a disproportionate amount of capital. To address this, ING has made portfolio choices based on market leadership, capital intensity, return on capital, funding needs, earnings contribution, and the overall coherence of the group.[2]

RESTRUCTURING

ING Group announced its major restructuring plan on October 26, 2009. This plan was a pivotal component of ING's "Back to Basics" program, aimed at simplifying the company's structure and operations in response to the global financial crisis. A key element of the restructuring involved the complete separation of ING's banking and insurance operations, including its investment management business. The company committed to divesting all insurance and investment management activities, as well as ING Direct US and certain Dutch mortgage and consumer lending operations, by the end of 2013.

After heavy negotiations with the EC, the restructuring plan received final and formal approval from the EC on November 18, 2009. This approval was necessary under EU rules for companies that had received state aid during the financial crisis. The EC's endorsement also cleared the way for ING to proceed with the issuance of core Tier 1 securities to the Dutch State and the implementation of the IABF.

Subsequently, on November 25, 2009, ING's shareholders approved the strategic decisions outlined in the restructuring plan, including the separation of banking and insurance operations and a rights issue of up to €7.5 billion to facilitate early repayment of state aid.

Already before these strategic moves, ING announced several internal restructuring measures in 2009 to streamline operations and reduce costs. For instance, on January 26, 2009, the company announced a global workforce reduction of 7,000 jobs as part of its efforts to lower operating expenses by €1 billion.

Other restructuring efforts included the announcement on July 1, 2009, to consolidate its three Dutch insurance brands, Nationale-Nederlanden, RVS, and ING Insurance, into a single entity under the Nationale-Nederlanden brand. This move aimed to streamline operations and resulted in the planned reduction of 800 jobs over three years.[3]

These restructuring initiatives were integral to ING's strategy to navigate the challenges posed by the financial crisis, restore financial stability, and position the company for sustainable growth.

In the end, ING sold more than fifty business units, generating €40 billion in proceeds. Part of that went toward repaying the government and the rest toward improving its capital position.

OPERATIONAL PAIN

The restructuring took an operational toll on the business and an emotional toll on the employees.

Operationally, it wasn't easy to divest. Although it sounds simple to say, "Go sell your insurance companies and asset managers," the reality was that nobody was buying. The whole world was in shambles. There were no financial institutions healthy enough to make acquisitions.

On the insurance side, buyers viewed the asset composition of insurance companies as opaque. Part of the financial crisis was caused by insurance firms with unclear or risky assets (remember AIG). The lack of transparency killed demand.

Asset managers weren't attractive either. In a crisis, there isn't much to invest. It's not a growth business in downturns.

ING also had a large real estate development unit that had lost a lot of money.

In 2011, ING sold ING Direct US to Capital One as part of the EC restructuring agreement. ING sold ING Direct Canada to Scotiabank in 2012. This was a strategic choice, as there was no wholesale banking business there to generate assets.

All of it hurt, but it showed the world ING was committed to correcting its wrongs and making things right.

CORPORATE SURVIVAL MODE

People understood the stakes. They had to save the company. That meant going *dramatically* back to basics on safeguarding: capital and liquidity, reducing costs, and risk. Everything became very corporate, very technical.

That continued for a long time. The Executive Board stayed focused on repaying the government and ensuring ING was viable and stable so it would never need state capital support again. While the board focused on the big picture, country managers were on the ground, working directly with clients around the world, many of whom were also in crisis.

ING couldn't afford to turn inward. As the global economy reeled, our clients needed support just as much as we did. Helping them recover became part of our own recovery.

At the time, I was CEO of ING Belgium and Luxembourg.

All country managers had to cut risk, costs, and leverage while serving clients. As part of the restrictions put in place by the EC, ING was not allowed to compete on price for retail clients and small and medium enterprises (SME). ING couldn't make any acquisitions that might delay repayment to the Dutch State.

ING was divesting and laying off. There was a lot of uncertainty for the employees.

WILL BANKING SURVIVE?

Even four years after the 2008 financial crisis, trust in the system had not been restored.

New waves of regulation were on the horizon. In Europe, the idea of a European Banking Union emerged, good news for ING strategically, but it came alongside relentless pressure to restructure. Inside the financial industry, everyone understood this broader context. Each institution was battling its own version of the same crisis. It was extremely stressful, but internally, the tone wasn't as emotionally charged as the public discourse. That emotion played out in politics, the press, and the broader public.

At the time, banks were overwhelmed. They were recovering from reputational damage, recapitalizing, and just trying to stay afloat. There was no room to modernize, no capacity to rebuild infrastructure, no energy to evolve. They were locked in crisis management mode.

Governments were also struggling. The sovereign debt crisis, particularly in Greece, put massive pressure on the eurozone. If Greece had left the EU, others might have followed. The euro's stability was on the line.

This was the world ING was operating in: restructuring fatigue, intense regulatory oversight, and public pressure, just as a new generation of competitors began to rise.

WHY THE CRISIS PAVED THE WAY FOR FINTECHS

While traditional banks were busy recovering, a quiet revolution was happening in tech.

Between 2010 and 2012, neobanks began doing what ING Direct had done (using tech to disrupt the industry and making banking simpler and faster) but with current accounts instead of savings. They branded themselves as super-digital banks:

"Do everything in an app."

When ING Direct launched in the late 1990s, the proposition was deliberately simple. We positioned ourselves as the "second bank," a place where customers could earn better savings rates because we avoided the heavy infrastructure costs of branches, ATMs, and domestic payment networks. It was a strategic choice, not a technological limitation. Even then, we were already expanding into current accounts in several markets, and features like checks were only ever relevant in the United States.

By the time I stepped into the role of CEO in October 2013, the world had shifted; I expected that nearly every financial product could be delivered faster, cheaper, and more conveniently through a smartphone. The original ING Direct model had proven what was possible. Suddenly, neobanks could become the primary bank. That became the cornerstone of ING's strategy under my leadership: transforming ING from an internet savings bank into a full-service, digital-primary bank.

Neobanks pursued that same strategy, but they repeated ING's pre-crisis mistake. They were offering credit cards and some consumer loans, but they were growing mostly in current accounts and savings, so growth on both sides of the balance sheet was not in balance.

A stable bank needs to grow both sides of the balance sheet in sync, or at the same pace. Without that, they were walking into the same trap ING Direct US had fallen into, having to invest in assets that were not originated by themselves, like with Alt-A.

Fintechs were attacking the banking value chain piece by piece. Most started with payments: fully digital and easy to disintermediate. These models inserted themselves between customers and banks. Others entered from the commerce side; platforms like eBay, Shopify, and Amazon started their own payment tools.

This disintermediation was dangerous. Payments were one of the few daily interactions customers had with their banks; payment data would give banks insight into customer behavior, like spending habits, risk signals, and overconsumption. As fintechs claimed this space, banks would lose their ability to observe.

ING was still relying on outdated channels in markets where we were the incumbents (branches, relationship managers) while these apps threatened to outpace it. It seemed impossible for ING to catch up. Its tech stacks weren't ready. Meanwhile, fintechs were supported by innovation sandboxes and allowed to test products under lighter regulatory oversight.

Big Tech entered the space, too. Amazon, Google, and Apple—companies with capital, reach, digital know-how, and none of the regulatory drag—became a new force to reckon with.

The pressure came from both sides: small, agile fintechs funded by venture capital firms (VCs) and massive tech giants with existing customer trust.

It was the perfect storm. While traditional banks struggled to survive, as they regained societal trust, fintechs and digital giants raced ahead, reshaping the entire competitive landscape.

THE NEED FOR A CLEAR FUTURE

At that point, internally, people were worn down. Uncertainty was corrosive. ING was preparing companies for sale. It was streamlining them, cutting costs, and making them attractive to buyers. That meant more staff reductions and more restructuring. But the world was moving on.

ING hired professionals to execute the separation. Many had no history with ING, no loyalty, and limited understanding of its culture. Those people were shaping its future but were generally not expected to be part of it.

People on the ground felt increasingly disconnected. What was happening centrally was often necessary, but it did not always connect to their day-to-day reality or to the needs of their clients.

Everyone knew change was necessary, but not everyone agreed on how fast it should happen, what direction it should go, or the values used to get there.

What Jan did worked to save the bank. But restructuring is never popular. You cannot make everyone happy.

To understand the scale of what ING went through: before the crisis and bailout, it had 125,000 employees. By 2013 when I took over, it had 76,000.[4] That was not just a staff reduction: ING became a completely different company in four years.

It was exactly what needed to be done, but it left everyone drained. The people working there were desperate for a new life. But more restructuring needed to be done after I became CEO.

ING launched the IPO of NN Group in 2014, its European and Japanese insurance and investment operations, reducing its stake to 68 percent. It continued selling down its stake in Voya Financial, reaching 19 percent by year-end. The sale of ING Investment Management Taiwan to Nomura Asset Management was completed in April, and the sale of its 50 percent stake in ING-BoB Life to BNP Paribas Cardif closed in December. On November 7, 2014, ING completed the full repayment of the state aid. These actions marked a pivotal moment for ING, allowing it to focus fully on banking while exiting insurance and investment management and demonstrating its financial recovery and strategic clarity.

Sharing time between completing the remaining restructuring and building a future for the bank was emotionally challenging. Colleagues in one part of the organization were living with uncertainty about their future, while others were becoming re-energized by the opportunity to help build a digital bank.

ING was ready to move from restructuring to transformation, and that was my task as newly appointed CEO. For me, that responsibility didn't begin on my first official day in the role. It began months earlier.

CHAPTER 2

THE SUN RISES ORANGE

Vision without strategy is inspiration; strategy without execution is theory. Think Forward translated ambition into a disciplined, one-page framework (Strategy on a Page) that defined a customer promise, strategic priorities, and clarified enablers. When strategy is clear and consistent, it becomes the bridge between intention and performance. A framework is provided.

I'll never forget the day.

It was February 22, 2013, when my appointment as CEO of ING Group was announced. I was officially set to take over on October 1.

I had been with ING for twenty-two years. My background was in wholesale banking, and while I also had experience with retail, I hadn't been in the spotlight.

Between the time of the announcement and October 1, we completed several transactions: we sold our stake in Sul America, kicked off the Voya Financial IPO, sold our 49 percent stake in KB Life in Asia, and sold our Mexican mortgage business to Santander. While Jan was driving those deals, I was preparing.

After years focused on asset quality, capital, and restructuring, I started looking around: at iPhones, digitalization, what was happening in banking, and how fintechs were changing the game. It was like a breath of fresh air.

I began reading voraciously, thinking about how digital would transform banking and the relationship between banks and customers. While we had our heads down, the world had kept moving. Customer expectations had evolved. Technology had moved on. New competitors emerged.

We had to catch up.

On October 1, I officially became ING's CEO. I thanked Jan for his incredible commitment and leadership during what were undeniably the most challenging years in our company's history.

RESTRUCTURING VS. TRANSFORMATION

Transformation is hard. Restructuring, by comparison, is easy because it's tactical. You gather a group of people around a table, look at the numbers, and make decisions. It's a process driven by urgency, by a real, tangible problem. A part of the organization isn't healthy, or it's not profitable, so you act: lay people off, sell off parts of the business, or simplify the structure. It's difficult work, but it's direct. You know what needs to be done, and you go do it.

Transformation, on the other hand, is something else entirely. It takes time. And it's not just about changing the structure; it's about changing the people within it. Transformation starts with a vision of who we are today and who we need to become to succeed in the future. That's not something you fix with a spreadsheet. It means changing how people behave, what they value, what they're good at. It means asking them to learn new skills, let go of old habits, and take ownership of a new future. That kind of change happens from the inside out.

I inherited a business that was operational and functioning but had been reduced and simplified through necessary restructuring. That work had to be done to survive and repay the Dutch State. To do that, many units were sold to generate capital. That wasn't wrong. It was what was needed at the time.

But once survival was no longer the only goal, that's where transformation began, and my mindset kicked in. I'm a glass-half-full person. I don't just see challenges; I look for the opportunity in them. To do that effectively, I needed others to see those opportunities, too. Because once people see the opportunity, you can ask them to change: to think differently, to act differently, to upskill, reskill, and grow into what's needed next.

To truly transform, it takes at least three to five years; we needed to align on a vision, create a burning ambition to motivate people, define clear stages and milestones to track progress, and communicate that progress. It requires a compelling story and external proof points to inspire belief. It demands structural and governance changes, cultural and behavioral shifts, and the development of new capabilities and skills. Transformation takes conviction, discipline, consistency, and persistence.

That was the difference between restructuring and transformation. Restructuring is based on a need, on a platform that is burning; transformation is creating what you want to do and is based on a burning *ambition* that many share. Restructuring had helped us survive, but transformation would define who we could become.

We weren't just trying to fix the past anymore; we were ready to be different and shape the future.

PREPPING FOR CEO AND THE GLOBAL LISTENING TOUR

In the months leading up to the start of my tenure as CEO of ING, I split my time between restructuring, prepping for CEO, and developing ING's strategy; I went on a Global Listening Tour to get a full perspective on what was happening externally and internally at ING.

I met with business unit leaders and talented colleagues across all levels of the ING organization, well beyond the boardroom, to gather input and start shaping a vision for our future.

I also met with many CEOs of companies in different industries and asked feedback and input from several large investors in ING at the time.

I spent time with leading tech companies and universities. My goal was to gather ideas on how to transform ING from a bank reeling from the crisis and restructuring into a forward-looking financial institution ready to lead on the global stage.

As part of this tour, I also visited Silicon Valley, where I was invited to a dinner by Index Ventures. It was an intimate gathering with a partner and four CEOs of newly formed fintech startups. As we sat around the table, I naturally began asking questions.

"What do you do?" I asked one founder. "What are you trying to disrupt? And how are you planning to do that?"

About half an hour in, the person who had invited me leaned over and said, "Ralph, we didn't invite you here so you could ask us questions; we invited you so we could ask *you* questions."

I was caught off guard. "What do you mean?" I asked. "I'm representing a legacy institution, a big bank that's coming out of restructuring. Why would that be of interest to you?"

He looked at me and said, "We've done the analysis. Since the beginning of the internet era, only two financial players have successfully used the internet to build a sustainable business model. Most early digital initiatives flamed out or went bankrupt. But two survived: PayPal and ING Direct."

That moment really struck me. I was suddenly confronted with a strength we'd almost forgotten we had, something deeply embedded in ING's DNA. We had a history of using technology not just to improve banking but to fundamentally rethink it. ING Direct was a perfect example: a low-barrier, digitally native model that scaled successfully and stood the test of time.

THE FIVE KEY TAKEAWAYS FROM THE GLOBAL LISTENING TOUR

The Global Listening Tour generated key insights, creating a turning point for ING: the strategic shift toward becoming a tech-driven, future-ready bank.

1. THE WAKE-UP CALL: DINNER WITH INDEX VENTURES

There was this key moment during the dinner when I realized they were looking to ING for insight. That was the wake-up call: the outside world saw us as successful and having special skills, but internally, we had lost sight of that during the years of restructuring. It was a reminder that ING was a leader in digitalization.

2. LEARNING FROM APPLE: INTUITION AND INTEGRATION

The second major influence was my visit to Apple. They were putting the functions of Nokia, Blackberry email, and the iPod into one device, the iPhone, with a touchscreen that was completely intuitive. I was blown away by the potential for daily use beyond those core functions, and that's when I realized: banking is not only going to be accessible via touchscreen but also readily available in your pocket every moment of the day. I could see the iPhone was more than a phone; it was a vision for integration, simplicity, and user-centered design. It could be used for daily payments and enable a direct bank (like ING) to develop a primary relationship with our customers.

3. EXPONENTIAL THINKING AT SINGULARITY UNIVERSITY

The third insight came from visiting Singularity University, where we were introduced to the concept of exponential growth. Unlike the steady, linear progress most banks were used to, technology supports business growth, making it far more disruptive. You don't see the threat coming until it's already overtaken you.

In banking, we couldn't afford to be complacent. If we didn't act with urgency, someone else leaner, faster, more tech-enabled would disrupt us. It also sparked a realization: we already knew how to reach clients digitally. We just hadn't fully leaned into that potential.

That moment helped shift our mindset. We began to think and act like a digital company, tracking growth quarterly and focusing on scaling faster through technology. The goal wasn't just to keep up with change but to lead it.

4. BUILDING FAST AND SMART: GOOGLE'S PRETOTYPING APPROACH

The fourth moment came from Google. I was inspired by their front-to-back product and service development structure and the use of multifunctional teams. They constantly evolved their offerings through pretotyping (or "pretend-typing," as it is sometimes called), building something close to reality before full prototyping. They didn't do customer interviews, because opinions don't always reflect behavior. Pretotyping lets you observe how people behave. That's what matters. (More on this topic in Chapter 7: The New Way of Working.)

5. CULTURE AND EMPOWERMENT: THE CAMPUS MODEL

The fifth insight was cultural. All these companies, Apple, Google, the startups, work in campus-like environments. They empower their people to act, to create, and to innovate within a clear direction; their teams continually changed in composition. That's what I wanted to replicate at ING: to build a culture of empowerment. We needed to create that feeling and enable that way of working inside the bank.

A STRATEGY ROOTED IN EXTERNAL INSPIRATION

The five insights from my Silicon Valley trip became central to where we would take ING. They shaped our strategic development. We asked ourselves: *What's happening in the world? What do we need to do to stay competitive?*

It was a bold and consistent strategy that never mentioned a bank. I talked about fintechs, exponential growth, checking your account while waiting for your coffee at Starbucks (something that didn't exist at the time), and campus working models.

None of that is traditionally associated with banking, and that was the point. Leadership requires external inspiration.

LEARNING FROM DISRUPTION

Back in Silicon Valley, I heard how startups were leveraging new technologies to challenge even the largest companies. The lesson was clear: if you don't spot disruptive developments early enough, it's too late to defend against them.

Kodak is a classic example. They didn't see how fast digital photography was coming; they didn't adapt, and they ceased to exist. Disruption often stays under the radar until it breaks through, and by then, you're toast.

We need to disrupt ourselves
before something disrupts us.

SETTING ASPIRATIONS

WE NEED TO BECOME A BANK
WITHOUT A BALANCE SHEET.

WE NEED TO TRANSFORM INTO A TECH
COMPANY WITH A BANKING LICENSE.

We asked: *How can we be more than a traditional bank?*

1. Be number one in customer experience: We wanted to be so easy to deal with that clients would consistently rank us as number one in customer experience. That meant analyzing, simplifying, and constantly improving to deliver on a clear customer promise at the center of our strategy.

2. A bank without a balance sheet: We questioned whether we needed to have all products and solutions for our customers ourselves. Or could we rely on other players providing those through our platform? In a world that was being disrupted through disintermediating the client relationship, we needed to decide: Do we want to be the financial infrastructure (the tracks), or should we own the client experience and with that the client relationship (the train)?

3. Digital as the business model: Most banks used technology to help employees serve clients. We wanted to flip that: use technology to empower clients directly. Digital wasn't just there for support or efficiency; it was there for a unique user experience. It was our engine.

4. A tech company with a banking license: We wanted ING

to be seen not just as a bank but as a tech company with a banking license. This shift in identity reflected our ambition to lead with innovation. We didn't just want to adapt. We wanted to inspire.

THINKING IN EXPONENTIALS

To be more aspirational, we needed top talent and exponential thinking. We asked teams to think 10x, boldly and creatively. That mindset powered our transformation. It's what I hope this story inspires in others: big thinking, humility in service, and deep respect for the people we serve.

REBUILDING TRUST

During the financial crisis, public trust in banks collapsed. As a financial institution, we're integral to society, but we had to ask ourselves: *how do we get that trust back?*

It starts with doing our core job well, taking deposits, granting loans, managing risk. But trust requires more. It's about our broader role contribution. I had a strong belief that banks had a fundamental responsibility to help better society.

Two key commitments emerged:

- Financial Health: Helping customers manage their money and understand its value.
- Climate Impact: Supporting sustainability through our choices and financing.

These pillars guided how we rebuilt trust. Because trust isn't built through words; it's built through repeated experiences. Over time. And what you do should be authentic. That's what we set out to deliver, and our strategy needed to reflect that. (See Chapter 10: Impact at Scale.)

A SHIFT TOWARD HUMILITY

All this required ambition but also humility. After the Dutch State stepped in to rescue ING, there was a deeper awareness that we served the people and were meant to play a responsible role for society. That awareness sharpened our focus on the customer even more. We had to acknowledge a fundamental truth: banking is never a primary need. No one wakes up in the morning excited to make a payment or take out a mortgage. Banking is a means to an end. It's secondary, and it should be invisible when done well. Our job is to remove friction and make it effortless for people to do the things they really care about.

That realization brought clarity. We are not the heroes of our customers' stories; they are.

Even before the digital revolution, ING was always customer-first. Low-barrier banking wasn't something we discovered after the crisis; it was part of our DNA from the start. It came from our founding companies, Postbank for consumers and NMB to support the SME segment. That consistency helped us stay focused during the recovery. We didn't lose sight of who we were, and I believe that foundation needed to play a key role in our transformation.

HOW WE CREATED THE STRATEGY

During my global listening tour, including my visits to Silicon Valley, I realized that my first appointment needed to be the Head of Strategy. At the time, Dorothy Hill and I were traveling together to get feedback from investors. She was head of investor relations. We visited several ING shareholders, and as we talked, I explained where I thought things should go.

She said, "Well, if you're looking for a head of strategy, I would love to do that."

That's how it happened. I went to Jan and said, "Look, you're still in charge, but I really want her to take that role. Can she start working with me on this?" And she did.

Every Friday, no matter where I had been in the world, whether I was coming from an interview, a Silicon Valley visit, an internal conversation, one of my many client visits, or a meeting with one of the thirty CEOs I met with during that time, I'd come back and spend the afternoon in a strategy session. Dorothy would be there; Radboud Vlaar (a McKinsey partner); Peter Jong, Head of Communication and Branding; and Hein Knaapen, Head of HR. I would share what I saw, what I thought, what I observed. I wanted them to absorb my findings and impressions so I could bring them on that same journey, even though they weren't joining me on my trips.[5]

They had their jobs to do, of course, but I kept them close to the thinking, constantly playing back insights. That's what we did for five to six months before I officially became CEO.

Similar to a custom amongst ING staff functions, we called those Friday lunches "kroketten lunches," named after a Dutch snack. Topics included the five takeaways I mentioned earlier, but that was just one. Most of the time, we focused on the trends Dorothy analyzed: regulatory developments, technology shifts, new competitors, strategic implications. One recurring theme was purpose. I was a fan of Simon Sinek's book *Start with Why*, and I believed we had to start with it.

If we had this once-in-a-lifetime opportunity to start with a blank sheet of paper, literally, we should take it. Of course, we were inheriting legacy. But I pushed us to start as blank as possible in our thinking. What kind of company would we create if there were no constraints? Then we could work backward and ask, "Can we do that? Would that fit ING? And if so, how?"

STRATEGY, BRAND, CULTURE, AND TALENT: THE NONNEGOTIABLES

Connecting the dots was already happening around that table. I've always believed a CEO can't delegate three things: strategy, communication and brand/reputation, and talent and culture. That's why Peter represented communication and brand, Hein represented talent and culture, and Dorothy was strategy. These three areas are the essential dots a CEO must connect for consistency. That's always been my style. Intuitively, it just worked. And from the beginning, those three were in the room to reinvent banking.

THE WORKSTREAMS

It was clear that this strategy would not be written in isolation. During the summer leading up to my first day as CEO, we deliberately set up a series of workstreams already to explore the most critical questions facing ING. These were not abstract debates about the future of banking; they were focused, practical efforts to understand where we were strong, where we were vulnerable, and where we needed to change course.

These are four of the workstreams we focused on:

1. Customer Experience
2. Data Analytics
3. Operational Excellence and Simplification
4. Balance Sheet Optimization

Each workstream was led by people from inside the organization who knew the reality on the ground. They brought together perspectives from different countries, wholesale and retail businesses, and functions. They were asked to be honest (not diplomatic) about what was working and what was not.

What struck me was not just the quality of the analysis but the consistency of the signals. Across workstreams, similar themes emerged: fragmentation where we needed focus, complexity where we needed simplicity, and untapped potential where we needed to move faster. Customer experience highlighted the growing gap between what people expected in a digital world and what banks were delivering. Data analytics showed how much value was locked inside ING but also how siloed and underused that data still was. Operational excellence exposed how legacy processes and local variations created friction for customers and colleagues alike. Balance sheet optimization made it clear that strategic focus and discipline would be essential to fund growth and resilience at the same time.

Just as important was how this work was done. By involving talent from across the organization early, we made the strategy a shared endeavor. People could see their fingerprints on it. That built engagement, credibility, and ownership long before any formal decisions were announced. It also sent a clear signal: this transformation would not be imposed from the top. It would be built with the organization, not for it.

In hindsight, these workstreams did more than inform the strategy. They set the tone. They demonstrated that listening and facts mattered and that we were serious about turning insight into action. That foundation proved critical for everything that followed.

DISRUPTING YOURSELF BEFORE SOMEONE ELSE DOES

The first speech I gave to ING's top 200 was on September 29, 2013. That one was all about urgency. I focused on the trends reshaping industries through technology. Kodak. The music industry. These weren't just examples of companies struggling with tech adoption. These were examples of entire industries and value chains vanishing within two years because they failed to see the shift coming.

The point wasn't about using technology to improve what we do. It was about using technology to imagine a completely different business model. I made it clear: we had to be willing to disrupt ourselves before someone else did it for us. If we didn't dare to cannibalize our own business, we'd fall into the trap of incrementalism, using tech for gradual improvement instead of transformative change.

We already had ING Direct operating as a challenger brand in several countries. It gave us permission to embrace a more disruptive model and culture for the whole organization. Small-screen banking, an intuitive digital experience, and straight-through processes; these were our opportunities to leap forward. We had to be bold.

As a sign of boldness, my presentation was supported by images only; no numbers, no tables, no text. A complete departure from the past.

THE NUN, THE POPE, AND THE DISAPPEARANCE OF CAMERAS

To bring the urgency of disruption to life, I used a series of vivid examples: images and moments that made the future feel immediate.

I showed a photo from the 2013 papal inauguration: St.

Peter's Square packed with people. Everyone was taking pictures with their phones, not cameras. The image captured the shift in real time. Then I pivoted: where did the camera business go?

I followed it with the Lady Gaga example: how she built one of the most passionate fan communities using social media, direct engagement, branding, and community strategy to create extremely loyal followers and bypass traditional gatekeepers. I asked: where did the record business go?

This was all about how new technology was reshaping everything. These industries didn't evolve, they were overtaken, rapidly disrupted by unknown new parties. And I made the case that the same could happen to us: neobanks were set up; Apple, Google, and Amazon were looking at entering the payments world; embedded finance in e-commerce was introduced. If we didn't stay close to consumers, be where they are, and know how they act, or use technology not as an enabler but as a dif-ferentiator, we'd be next.

FROM TALK TO ACTION

The next day in that weekend, the findings of the workstreams were presented. That was intentional. I did not want to arrive with a fully formed strategy and ask the organization to execute it. I wanted to arrive in the middle of the conversation. The workstreams ensured that the strategy was already being shaped by the people who would ultimately have to bring it to life.

Then the top 200 was asked to work on questions like these: How do we see technology shaping banking? What are the trends we need to respond to? What should ING do next, also in view of the workstream findings?

That created a moment of countdown. The top 200 were both exhausted and energized: tired from the ongoing restructuring, knowing we still had work ahead, completing the IPO of NN Group (July 2, 2014) and fully repaying the Dutch State. But they were also excited. I had inspired them to think forward…literally. I encouraged them to hold their heads high, be proud of what we'd accomplished, and believe in the future we could build. I asked them to look ahead to future trends and to imagine building a bank no one had built before.

That energy carried through the night. On the eve of September 30, just before my official first day as CEO, they called me back from my hotel room to join them on the dance floor. They wanted to count down the final ten seconds with me.

"There was such a need; it was like opening the windows and suddenly everyone had oxygen, giving people hope and optimism, making them feel like things were going to change."

—DOROTHY HILL, FORMER ING HEAD OF STRATEGY

A SYMBOL AND A MESSAGE

The next day, I closed the conference by acknowledging our journey.

"We've come through major restructuring, and more is still ahead."

But I reminded everyone: "The sun rises orange every day. Yes, we face threats from new competitors and technologies. But if anyone can turn those threats into opportunities, it's us. The sun rises orange every day."

That morning, we gave everyone a special alarm clock in their hotel room. Instead of a buzzer, it used a soft orange light to wake them up. It was a symbol: the sun rises orange every day. They took those clocks home as a reminder that however hard it gets, we're capable of leading this transformation.

"The sun rises orange every day" also nicely connected to our brand color.

That symbolic close to the conference marked a turning point, not just in mood but in momentum. From that moment forward, our strategy wasn't just an internal rallying cry; it became the foundation of a new public narrative, one that would show up in our numbers, our communications, and our culture.

THE CONSISTENT NARRATIVE

From October 1, 2013, we entered five months of strategy development; the workstreams continued. We had biweekly buy-in sessions with the executive team and regular presentations to the board.

We had to develop two sides of the same story:

- The content side: what we were going to do, what our priorities were, and how countries would be involved.
- The investor side: because the strategy also had to appeal to the market. I couldn't just present on a Capital Markets Day that we'd use tech to disrupt the world. Investors don't buy stock on disruption per se. They want to understand the financials.

So, alongside developing the internal strategy and inspiring people with the right priorities, we also had to make a clear financial promise to the outside world, especially to shareholders. We needed to show where this would take us financially. How would these moves lead to sustainable returns, returns beyond the cost of capital? We needed to demonstrate that we would continue the restructuring and start the transformation, generate capital, repay the Dutch State, *and* set the tone for the future of banking. At that time, we were still under state support. We didn't repay the last of it until November 7, 2014.

DEFINING SUSTAINABLE SHARE

As we analyzed our business units in different countries, we believed that success was not determined only by financial performance and market share. In some markets, especially with ING Direct, we were still relatively small, but we were punching far above our weight in terms of customer loyalty and brand awareness.

With the Direct model, we believed we would be able to achieve strong financial performance at a smaller scale, because the business model was lower cost. For our portfolio review, we took a more holistic view with a concept called Sustainable Share.

1. Are We Relevant to Our Customers, Primary and Nonprimary?

Do we have the daily banking relationship with our customers, or are we their secondary bank?

User experience and net promoter score (NPS) had to be top tier. NPS is a customer advocacy metric. Those metrics are leading indicators for future growth, and more importantly, the feedback keeps you close to your customers. Even if your financial performance is poor, if you've built strong customer rapport, at least you have something to work with.

We didn't only want to be number one in the NPS but lead the competition by ten points. Other variables we measured were growth in number of customers, percentage of customers that are primary relationships, and the cross-buy of products.

2. Are We Relevant as a Market Player?

Elements like brand awareness, consideration to buy, market share, and market position are part of this. Do we have meaningful market share? Do we have pricing power? Can we differentiate? Because if you have poor financial performance and no way to shift the market, there's no future for you.

3. Do We Have a Sustainable Balance Sheet?

Do we operate as a full bank? Do we offer all the products? What is our net interest margin? Do we manage an integrated balance sheet? Do we need cross-border funding? Our local liquidity position, loan-to-deposit ratio, and retail versus wholesale funding are crucial elements for each unit.

4. Return of the Unit

What's the actual return on equity (ROE) of the unit in question? What is the minimum ROE set for that activity in that country, the percentage of noninterest income to total income, and cost-to-income ratio?

"REINVENTING BANKING"

When I presented our plan to the Supervisory Board on January 16, 2014, the title said it all: "Reinventing Banking."

We weren't going back. We were moving forward, boldly, differently, confidently. Society had changed. So had our customers. Technology gave us the tools to evolve.

We brought everything together to create something new.

We used unexpected ideas to create a new kind of bank. That's where many of my one-liners came from: "A tech company with a banking license." "A bank without a balance sheet."

Explaining to the team and colleagues that we as bankers play a supporting role in the life or business of our customers came as a bit of a shock.

It was no longer about owning the product; it was about the experience. *It isn't about the tracks; it's about the train.* Whether we provided the mortgage or processed the payment didn't matter. What mattered was keeping a direct interaction with the customer.

Losing direct contact with our customers would make us dependent on others. To stay in control of our own destiny, we had to prioritize the customer experience. As a digital- and direct-first bank, we operated largely without branches or relationship managers in many markets. That meant we needed robust data analytics to anticipate client needs and manage risks.

At the same time, we had to move closer to where customers' primary needs were being met: in e-commerce, through real estate agents, in SME procurement, accounting, and beyond. We needed to play an invisible yet indispensable role in the value chain, whether it was purchasing a product or making an investment.

We didn't want to be limited by what ING had been or by the constraints of restructuring. We were a bank, yes, but we wanted to dream beyond that. We wanted to build something new.

And ING had already pioneered something new with ING Direct.

We didn't have branches. We offered savings accounts online, gave people better rates, and kept costs low. That wasn't just using tech to improve what we did; it was building a new kind of bank. Now we wanted to go further and build a digital bank with primary relationships.

THE POWER OF SIMPLICITY

If you can't summarize the strategy on one page, how can you expect 54,000 people to remember it?

My chairman always emphasized the importance of simplicity in strategy communication. If we wanted to be successful in delivering our strategy, we had to make things simple. That applied across the board:

- Our processes had to be simple.
- Our products had to be simple.
- Our client interactions had to be intuitive and simple.
- And we had to communicate in simple terms: short, sharp, clear.

That's how the idea of Strategy on a Page came to life. I told the entire team they must come up with something we can summarize on one page. That's what we need.

A FIRST FOR ING

This was unique for ING. In all my years there, we'd never had our strategy delineated on one page. It was usually buried in a forty-page document that very few people could explain.

So, for buy-in, especially in a company with so many different people and perspectives, it was essential that everyone could subscribe to the same page. Literally. If it's one page, it's something people can remember, internalize, and rally around.

Getting to that one-page strategy wasn't easy. In a culture like ours, with layers of compromise and broad perspectives, it took an enormous amount of effort to get to the essence. It was a journey. We sharpened the pencil again and again, refining the language, stripping down the purpose, removing unnecessary words, and zeroing in on the core.

That iterative, focused process of distilling, clarifying, and aligning is as much a part of the story as the strategy itself. And it creates the necessary buy-in for execution, too.

"We were very deliberate about making the strategy development process inclusive. The core strategy team worked alongside colleagues from internal communications, external communications, media relations, investor relations, branding, and HR. Through a series of design thinking workshops, we co-created the Strategy on a Page. That shared creation meant shared commitment, and it ensured the strategy was communicated clearly and consistently across every audience."

—DOROTHY HILL, FORMER ING HEAD OF STRATEGY

When people are not involved in the creation process, there's a tendency to tweak the messaging and "adapt" to each audience, and that's what we wanted to avoid. We needed consistency in messaging for all audiences to be clear and have impact.

I remember when I presented Strategy on a Page, I told everyone: "This is it: nothing more, nothing less. This is our strategy, these are our priorities, and this is what we want you to act on. Print it out and hang it next to your bathroom mirror or put it on your pillowcase so you see it when you wake up.

Use it as a placemat at breakfast or a mouse pad at your desk. Look at it every day and compare your planned activities with it.

"If your work isn't aligned with the strategy, change your activities. Talk to your team leader, and either adjust what you're doing, or have them explain how your role fits in. Every one of you matters on this journey. You all have a role to play in building a different kind of bank."

THINK FORWARD, OUR STRATEGY ON A PAGE

On March 31, 2014, we had our Capital Markets Day. We launched the Think Forward strategy, our long-term vision and transformation plan, to the outside world. The culmination of Think Forward was the one-page document we called Strategy on a Page. It took everything, our purpose, our customer promise, our strategic priorities, and our enablers, and condensed it into a single, clear, communicable framework.

1. PURPOSE

Why we exist, what we're here to do.

2. CUSTOMER PROMISE

How do we make banking as simple as possible and available everywhere, empower our clients, and keep getting better? Not as a slogan but as a set of very concrete commitments about how banking should feel in people's lives:

- Clear and Easy: Banking is already complex. Our job is not to add to that complexity but to absorb it on behalf of the customer. If something can be explained more simply, designed more intuitively, or completed with fewer steps, then we have an obligation to do so. Complexity inside the bank is our problem, not the customer's.
- Anytime, Anywhere: That means mobile and 24/7. People do not organize their lives around bank opening hours anymore. They manage money in the same moments they manage the rest of their lives: on the train, between meetings, late at night. If we want to be relevant, we have to be present where and when people need us, not when it is convenient for the institution.
- Empowering: We are very clear about this. The customer is in the driver's seat. Our role is not to tell people or companies what to do but to give them the data, insights, and tools to make better decisions themselves. If banking is done well, it stays in the background and enables those moments to happen smoothly. That mindset, peer-to-peer, not hierarchical, has long been part of ING's DNA, and this promise makes it explicit.
- Keep Getting Better: Digital is never finished. Learning, iter-

ating, and improving have to be continuous. If we see a way to make something faster, simpler, or more intuitive, we commit to doing it. We celebrate removing a single swipe in the app. We celebrate eliminating an unnecessary screen. Those are not marginal gains; they are proof points that we are taking friction out of people's lives, one interaction at a time.

Our strategy places user experience at the center, alongside financial performance and risk management.

The customer promise becomes a decision filter. It guides priorities, shapes trade-offs, and aligns teams across retail and wholesale banking. It is how purpose translates into action, and how strategy shows up in the daily experience of millions of people.

3. STRATEGIC PRIORITIES

Once our ambition was clear, we needed to be equally clear about what we would prioritize and what we would not. Strategy only works when it translates into a small number of focused choices that guide daily decisions across a large organization. These priorities are not abstract aspirations. They are practical answers to a simple question: *what must ING do exceptionally well to remain relevant in a rapidly changing digital world?*

- Earn the Primary Relationship: We want ING to be the main bank in a customer's life or business, the one they trust, rely on, and use most often. In a digital world where switching is easy, relevance matters. If we are not the primary relationship, we will become interchangeable.
- Develop Analytic Skills: We need to use data to better understand our customers and anticipate their needs, not

only describe what had already happened. We have access to enormous amounts of data, but turning that data into insight at scale is essential if we want to become more personal and more relevant.

- Increase the Pace of Innovation: We have to move faster. That means testing ideas quickly, learning from real customer behavior, and improving continuously rather than relying on slow, large-scale launches. Customer expectations are evolving rapidly, and speed is a necessity, not a luxury.
- Think Beyond Traditional Banking: We stop defining ourselves by products and start focusing on customer needs and specific moments in life and business. If we continue to think only in terms of traditional banking, we will miss where relationships and value are moving. We need to be where our customers will be.

Taken together, these priorities force us to shift how we think about banking. Relevance becomes more important than reach. Insight matters more than information. Speed outweighs perfection. Customer needs replace product definitions as our starting point. This is not about adding more initiatives; it is about sharpening our focus so everything we do reinforces the kind of bank we want ING to become.

4. ENABLERS

Strategic priorities alone do not create change. Without the right foundations, even the best strategy remains theoretical. To make our ambitions real, we need enablers that translate intent into execution, with capabilities and behaviors that allow the organization to move faster, operate more reliably, and take ownership at every level:

- Simplify and Streamline: We reduce unnecessary complexity in products, processes, and systems. Complexity creates friction for customers, slows the organization down, and can lead to compliance issues.
- Operational Excellence: We focus on delivering consistently, reliably, and efficiently every day. Trust in banking depends on doing the basics right, without exceptions.
- Performance Culture: We emphasize clear ownership, accountability, and follow-through. Empowerment only works when people take responsibility for outcomes.
- Lending Capabilities: We strengthen our lending capabilities by improving credit decision-making through better data, analytics, and processes. Lending remains core to ING's role in the economy and to sustainable growth. We should never be dependent on others to generate our assets, like we experienced buying Alt-A mortgages.

These enablers are not support functions operating in the background; they are the engine of transformation. By simplifying how we work, strengthening our operational discipline, reinforcing accountability, and modernizing our core lending capabilities, we create the conditions for strategy to scale. This is where vision meets reality and where transformation becomes sustainable rather than temporary.

FROM PURPOSE TO EXECUTION

This book covers all components of the transformation as indicated in the below framework, not in strict sequence or isolated by chapter but where they best serve the story. It also does not delve into ING's operational key results (OKRs) or key performance indicators (KPIs); the focus is on the choices, behaviors, and leadership decisions that shaped the transformation.

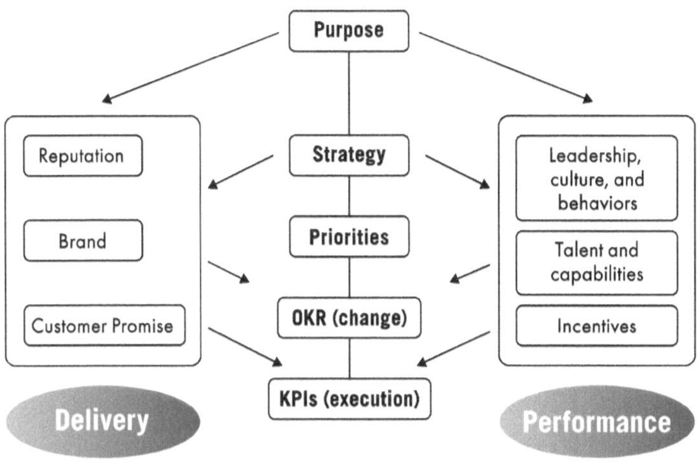

One of the most important reasons this transformation was successful is that we connected the dots, clearly and intentionally. That connection started at the top, with our purpose. From there came vision, and from vision came strategy. These three components form the top of the framework. They were essential but not enough on their own. What makes you different is what happens next, how you implement it. That's the bottom half of the framework. This is where we move from concept to execution. We identified a set of strategic priorities, and for each one we defined specific OKRs. Those OKRs are what we used to track execution and progress. Then we connected those OKRs to KPIs that could be measured. For example, one of our OKRs was "simplify client experience," and the corresponding KPI was becoming number one in NPS.

If the top half of the framework is about conception, the

bottom half is about execution. That's the vertical axis of my framework.

But most companies have a strategy, and many of them have a purpose statement. They may even have a plan to execute. But how many succeed in execution?

About the horizontal axis: on the outside, you've got how the strategy translates externally, your reputation, your brand, and how you deliver your customer promise. At ING, that meant rebuilding trust, standing for simple, empowering banking, and delivering a user experience that was easy to navigate. This set expectations and conditions as to the strategic priorities, OKRs, and KPIs. Hence the arrows toward them.

But internal alignment matters just as much. That's where we focused our energy. We activated the execution through behavior, values, communication, and ways of working.

We used culture/behavior as the bridge between vision and execution. Hence the arrows toward OKRs and KPIs. We embedded the transformation into everyday actions so that it didn't stay conceptual. It became part of how we operated, hired, led, and served. That's what made the strategy stick and why customers started to experience a different ING.

On the inside, we had to change the culture and introduce the Orange Code to model new behaviors. We wanted to shape a culture that was observable, so we needed to make the expected behaviors explicit.

We had to evolve our talent and capabilities. For example, we no longer needed as many branch tellers as possible, but we did need engineers, people who could build digital solutions. You can't train a branch teller into a software engineer. You must rethink the skillset entirely. And then we had to reinforce the right behaviors with the right incentives so our people were motivated and supported in doing what the strategy demanded.

That's the framework. One axis moves from conception to execution and the other from inside to outside. Both are essential. And it's only when you align those dimensions that transformation becomes real, not just a strategy document but a living, breathing transformation in how the organization operates and how the customer experiences it.

To guide you through the application of the framework and its components, every chapter will start with an image of the framework and will highlight the components discussed within.

A NEW NARRATIVE

When we launched our new strategy, it marked a clear shift in how we positioned ourselves both internally and externally. If you compare our annual reports from 2013 and 2014, the difference is striking. The 2013 report was still focused on restructuring. But by 2014, the tone had shifted toward aspiration. It was no longer about what we were trying to fix; it was about our clients and who we wanted to become.

That aspiration had to show up in how we measured ourselves. One of the most important signals was customer growth. If we truly believed we were doing something different and valuable, then we should see that reflected in market share. In 2014, we started reporting customer growth more explicitly.

We took the same approach with the number of primary clients. We wanted to prove to the world that if we truly understood our clients' needs, using data analytics, and approached them with timely, relevant digital offers, we could show that even a digital-only bank could build fully fledged, primary client relationships.

We started to more prominently report on NPS externally, which became one of our KPIs. It compares the number of clients who are true advocates of your brand to those who are detractors, those who are dissatisfied or likely to leave. When you have a higher proportion of advocates, you're more likely to grow organically. That's why NPS is considered a leading indicator in business terms; it gives you a window into future growth potential.

If you're number one in NPS in a country, and you maintain that lead, you will gain new customers over time. But it can't just be a promotional spike, offering a free credit card or a temporary rate drop or rate hike (on savings). That's not sustainable, and it's not authentic. NPS must be earned through consistent delivery on your customer promise. And that promise was clearly defined in our Strategy on a Page.

In 2014, we started tracking how well we were delivering across the four areas of the customer promise. When done consistently and authentically, this drove a higher NPS, which in turn supported long-term customer growth.

During my time as CEO of ING, from 2013 to 2020:

- Customers grew from 31.8M to 39.3M.
- Primary customers grew from 7.9M to 13.9M (10.6M are mobile-primary customers).
- We were almost consistently number one in NPS in most of the countries where we had a consumer bank.

I was proud to see that in 2014 we ranked first in NPS in nine of the eleven countries where we operated as a consumer bank. That was a clear signal we were headed in the right direction. And it wasn't just our customers who were responding; our employee engagement score hit 75 percent, which was also a meaningful sign of internal alignment and morale.

Looking back, 2014 was the year our transformation started

to take root. The numbers told a story. But more importantly, they showed that our aspiration was turning into real performance.

<h2 style="text-align:center">THE CULTURAL DIVIDE</h2>

Not everyone could, or would, get on board. A shift in identity like this is clarifying. It separates those who align with the vision from those who don't. Some saw the future and wanted to build it. Others couldn't, or wouldn't, let go of the past. They left soon after.

That tension is powerful. If people don't truly want to be part of what's next, their energy drags everything down. Culture is never just one chapter of a transformation. It's the throughline. The undercurrent. It seeps into every part of the company.

And it all begins with a leadership decision, a bold vision, and the willingness to let the divide happen. It was important to create as much buy-in as possible. It may take longer at the beginning but will hold better when executing. The believers stay and become ambassadors.

Some employees resisted the idea that banking could be something radically new. Digital-first? Digital-only? Reimagined from the ground up? That wasn't just unfamiliar; it was uncomfortable. For some, the instinct was to retreat to what they knew: the clichés, the legacy, the "old ING."

But we couldn't lead from the rearview mirror. Our identity had to evolve. We had to shift from loss and fatigue into pride, pride in a new kind of company with a new kind of story.

And we did. Within two years, the media was following us closely and seeing us as a resurrection story. A digital-first pioneer. A global bank with startup energy.

That was something people could believe in again. Something they could say proudly at birthday parties. We were back, with a new identity, not a recycled one.

REBUILDING WITH PURPOSE

Getting the language right was only part of the equation. We had to fill the story with meaning, something that could inspire belief and unite the organization behind the change.

This is why purpose became central. Because once you ask, "Why are we here?" you start a different kind of journey. That's what we needed.

Later, when we asked employees what ING should become, the response was powerful. The question was alive across the organization. Of course, people looked to leadership to shape the answer. But the question itself, that lived everywhere. And it shaped our path forward.

That dinner in Silicon Valley was more than a wake-up call; it was a reminder of who we already were. ING had disrupted the industry before, and now we had the chance to do it again but bigger, bolder, and on our terms. Think Forward motivated and reignited the leadership, boosting confidence that we could lead the disruptions in banking. Think Forward was the theme of our first strategy launch and became the rallying cry for a new identity and a new kind of bank.

We weren't just recovering from the past; we were setting the tone for a future only we could lead. And at the center of that future, driving every choice and every change, was a single, animating question: why are we here? That's where the next chapter begins.

THE POWER OF PURPOSE

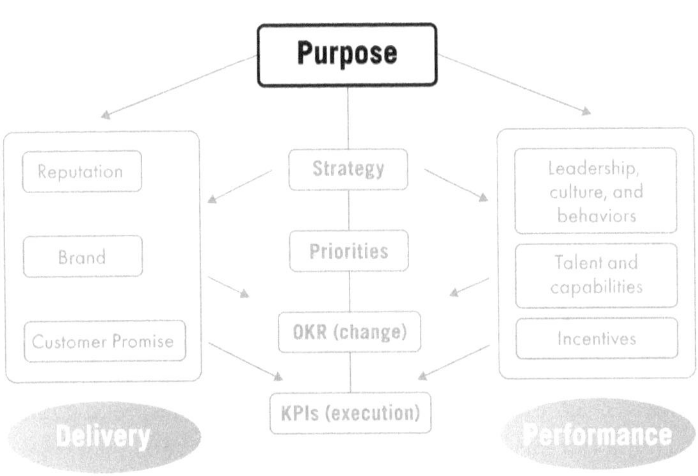

Purpose is not a slogan; it is the anchor that gives strategy meaning and direction. Without a clear "why," decisions become fragmented, dilemmas unsolved, culture drifts, and short-term pressures take over. By defining our purpose as empowering people to stay a step ahead in life and in business, we gave ING a compass that aligned customer focus, societal responsibility, and long-term performance.

Purpose is the reason people show up every day and believe their work matters.

As the dust settled from the financial crash, ING found itself in the middle of an identity crisis. Banks were broadly criticized after 2008 and 2009; there was a widespread global debate about the role of banks, and ING took an especially hard hit in the Netherlands.

The main sentiments around the world were: *What should a bank do? How can a bank serve society?*

That same conversation was happening *inside* the bank, because the ING team genuinely desired to contribute to something meaningful. At our core, we all want to be valued and make a difference. The team at ING was no different. We needed a reason, other than our paycheck, to get out of bed in the morning.

We needed a purpose.

A SILICON VALLEY BUZZWORD?

Purpose isn't something made up; it isn't a tagline or marketing slogan. It's already there, embedded in a company's DNA, waiting to be made visible so it can guide decisions and help people navigate dilemmas.

The journey to define ING's purpose started with my appreciation for Simon Sinek's work on the power of "why." Around that time, his book *Start with Why* had become hugely influential, and "purpose" was becoming a bit of a buzzword in the corporate world. Whether it was McKinsey, HR consultants, or internal strategy teams, everyone was talking about it.

At the time, 2013, some banks and financial institutions came out with purpose statements. Many felt like calls for world peace or "creating value for all stakeholders"—very generic.

We wanted to identify something specific and true to ING. That is why it is the starting point of my framework as well.

From the very beginning, the management team and I were convinced ING needed a purpose that captured what we already believed we were doing and the value we brought to society.

This wasn't about *inventing* our "why." It was about *uncovering* it.

We all agreed that's where we had to start.

Of course, we had cynics who said, "Write whatever you want on the walls. Purpose is just trendy right now." These are the same people who say, "If it doesn't make more money, why should we care?"

That skepticism was more common in wholesale banking (my background). These folks tend to focus on whether something drives shareholder value. If ING's purpose was simply a feel-good message, they'd say, "Fine. Make a poster, but don't bother us with it. What's the point?"

During my speech, in the weekend of March 29 and 30, 2014, when I presented the Think Forward strategy to the top 200, I made it very clear and addressed this: "Purpose is the point."

It's what makes us authentic. It's our strength in what we do.

These cynics needed further convincing. We showed them research from McKinsey showing that companies with a clear purpose outperformed those without one.

When you tap into the real strengths and DNA of your people, everything becomes more focused, more powerful, and more valuable.

> *"Ralph succeeded in bringing his people with him because he genuinely believed the company had a higher purpose."*
>
> —RUSS PINNEY, MANAGING DIRECTOR, TWOFISH
> CREATIVE ADVERTISING AGENCY

HOW CAN WE STAY TRUE TO OUR DNA?

I felt strongly about specifically defining ING's purpose from the beginning. We needed to shift focus back to the customer, and having a clear, grounded purpose was essential to that transition.

I remember during one of the Friday lunch meetings when Dorothy asked, "Why are we here? What's this all about?"

I leaned forward, nodding. "Exactly. Purpose must be central to our transformation."

"Too many companies have a strategy, a purpose, and a brand promise that don't sound like they belong to the same organization. They were developed separately by different departments. We can't make that mistake. We need to be very consistent."

She agreed. "It should be something everyone can use as a kind of North Star, where they can ask, 'Is what I'm doing contributing to our purpose?'"

We looked for examples of where this had worked at ING in the past, and ING Direct US stood out. "Save your money" was clear and relevant, especially in a market with one of the highest levels of consumer debt in the world. It spoke to something larger.

"We need something broader," I said. "It has to work for the *entire* bank, retail and wholesale banking, and still feel authentic."

ING's purpose had to speak to entrepreneurs, CFOs, and large enterprises, too. Something that could stretch across the business while staying true to our DNA.

The next question was: where do we start?

DEFINING ING'S PURPOSE

Before identifying ING's purpose, we asked ourselves three fundamental questions:

1. *What do our customers truly need?* We looked across markets, Belgium, Australia, the Netherlands, Germany, and searched for insights that were consistent and universal. Purpose had to start with the customer.
2. *What makes us different?* Not just in product or pricing but in how we show up, our values, our approach, and the experience we deliver.

3. *What role do we play in society?* Beyond profits, how can ING contribute to a better world?

We noticed that many banks had started with that last question, societal role, and completely missed the point about customers. That's where we were different. We believed a strong purpose had to sit at the intersection of all three. Not a slogan, not a campaign, but a real expression of who we are, what we stand for, and how we serve.

That clarity became the engine for everything that followed. Once we defined our purpose, we were ready to build strategy around it.

USING REAL DATA

The executive team and I agreed that ING's purpose was already embedded in its DNA. We didn't need to rely on intuition or sentiment; we could use *real data* to discover it.

We started with extensive customer research across all our markets to gather both positive and negative stories about banks.

Most of those stories were negative. People spoke about poor service, unreturned calls, confusing fees, and oversized bonuses.

But about 40 percent of the stories were positive, and those stood out. In them, the bank wasn't just a service provider; it played a pivotal role in the customer's life or business. Whether it was timely advice or a loan at the right moment, these stories showed what great banking could be.

We used narrative research to analyze the common themes in both types of stories. They became the foundation for reimagining what kind of relationship a bank could have with its customers.

The process was both rigorous and extensive. We worked with these customers for comments and feedback. We conducted external interviews, held internal wordsmithing sessions, and rewrote draft after draft. We tossed out versions that didn't work and started over again. We also wrote an introduction to the purpose statement to provide the right context for what it meant.

Throughout, I insisted the purpose statement had to be authentic, something that truly reflected what we at ING were already doing, without trying to be everything to everyone. It had to be understood by all our colleagues to live up to it.

I had seen how other companies crafted purpose statements that tried to tick every box: "We're here to create shareholder value by doing this and delivering that so our clients are happy and our staff is fulfilled."

These kinds of statements might be complete, but they don't feel like a genuine "why."

We wanted something that could cover all the bases without spelling them all out. It had to be naturally comprehensive, not exhaustively descriptive. That's what made it hard. We already knew our purpose, but putting it into one sentence that captured the essence of what we stood for took real work.

In the end, we landed on the idea of empowerment. When people spoke negatively about banks, it was usually about bonuses or other typical banking issues. When they spoke *positively*, it was about the progress banks enabled: buying a home, starting to save for their kids' college, or getting a loan to grow a company.

It wasn't about the product; it was about the moment. People wanted their bank to empower them to move forward.

That insight aligned naturally with ING's brand. As a direct bank, we had already attracted customers who wanted to oversee their own lives; people who valued autonomy and clarity. Empowerment wasn't a new idea for ING; it was already part of who we were, all the way back to Postbank. The research simply brought it into focus and gave us the confidence to build our purpose around it.

CRAFTING THE PERFECT STATEMENT

After extensive deliberation, we arrived at our purpose statement:

"Empowering people to stay a step ahead in life and in business."

This simple sentence contained layers of meaning that reflected our deepest values and approach. Breaking it down, the word "empowering" demonstrated that we saw ourselves as a secondary force rather than the primary actor. We weren't trying to be the star of our customers' stories; we were there to support them in whatever they were trying to achieve. This concept of empowerment went much deeper than simply providing digital tools that let people manage their own banking: it reflected our fundamental role as facilitators who helped people and companies accomplish their goals.

I remember standing on stage and saying, "Banks are not the economy's main players. *People* and *companies* are. Our *clients* are. No one wakes up in the morning thinking, *I want to make a payment.* People want to buy a coffee. Companies don't start their day thinking about taking out a loan; they're thinking about growth, change, and investment. To do those things, they need financing."

"Banking is necessary. Banks are not." Saying that, I saw the room shift. It looked as though people were thinking, *but we* are *important.*

Of course, we are. We facilitate. So, when we talk about facilitation, we must understand that people want their finances to be easy. Payments shouldn't take time. Transfers should be instant, even automatic.

That's true empowerment. Not just facilitating but doing it in a way that's invisible yet indispensable.

The choice to focus on "people" rather than specific stakeholder groups was deliberate. We weren't just empowering shareholders, staff, or clients; we were empowering *people,* regardless of their relationship to ING. Whether they were our colleagues, our clients, employees of our business clients, or members of society at large, our purpose was to empower people in whatever they were doing.

The final element, "in life and in business," ensured we captured the full scope of our client base. While it was natural to think about individual consumers staying ahead in their lives, we wanted our corporate customers to feel empowered, too. It was critical to acknowledge that we also helped businesses stay ahead in their competitive environments.

Given the scale and diversity of ING, it was tough, but I think we succeeded in crafting something that could carry the full complexity of our business. It may not have been as punchy or edgy as some would've liked, but it captured what we stood for.

ROLLING OUT THINK FORWARD ACROSS THE GLOBE

It took about six months for us to define ING's purpose. As described in Chapter 2, we had workstreams on customer experience, data analytics, operational excellence and simplification, and balance sheet optimization running in parallel.

The development of Think Forward took quite some time. Between the idea, the development of the strategy, announcement, and first steps of implementation, we needed almost a year.

At first, Hein and I thought a business school or leadership consultancy could guide us. We even ran a pilot. But it turned into gimmicks.

That's when we stopped everything and decided to focus on real internal business conversations, real clarity on what we wanted to achieve. Those discussions took months, but they gave Think Forward its foundation. That reset gave the strategy the buy-in and the space it needed to work.

"Think Forward" wasn't chosen by accident; we thought carefully about how to label it. The name ties directly to empowerment and helping people anticipate what's coming.

"Empowering people to stay a step ahead in life and in business."

As purpose and strategy came together in parallel, we

prepared to roll out Think Forward across all our markets. Ensuring our country managers and local colleagues had a clear, unified direction to rally behind, we captured the final articulation of the strategy in a single page, the so-called Strategy on a Page that I explained in the previous chapter.

To roll it out, we organized Think Forward workshops around the world. We started these workshops with a meditation exercise.

Yes, meditation...at a bank.

Senior leaders were asked to pause and really dream about the future of ING. It might sound cheesy, but it was powerful. At a global level, our top leaders were reflecting on the bank's future and ING's purpose. This kind of reflection had never happened before at ING, and it made a real impact.

TRULY EMBEDDING THINK FORWARD

In the first year alone, I traveled extensively to almost thirty countries to present Think Forward in person. We had video conferencing, but I made the choice to visit every location physically. I wanted the communication to be authentic.

It was also a sign of respect: this transformation mattered enough for me to show up and explain it myself.

In every country, I shared the strategy and then asked local leaders to return within three months to present how they would implement it in their market.

What would they do with it?

Defining our purpose gave us clarity. Rolling out Think Forward gave us direction. But neither would matter if the people leading ING continued to behave the way they always had.

Purpose can inspire. Strategy can guide. Leadership determines whether transformation becomes real.

CHAPTER 4

LEADING THE TRANSFORMATION

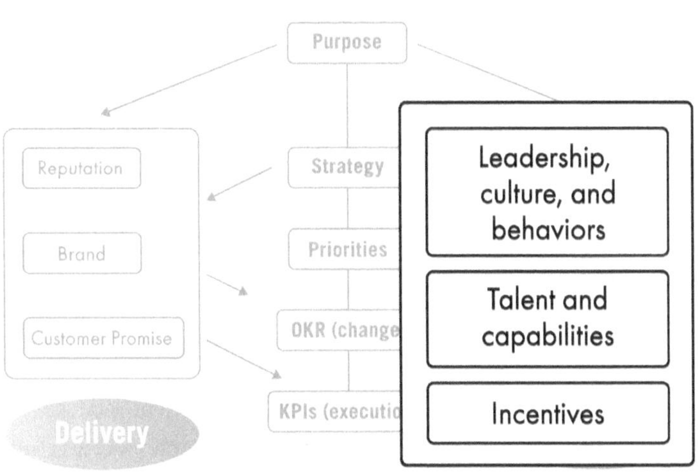

A transformation asks people to do new things, but first it asks leaders to lead in a new way. The shift from control and hierarchy to empowerment and ownership is not incremental; it forces a personal decision about alignment and identity. By redefining what leadership meant at ING, through the Leadership Council, the Think Forward Leadership Program, and aspirational performance expectations, we built the bench strength the strategy required. This gave room to develop a well-articulated culture, combining observable behaviors and values (the Orange Code) and supporting the execution on all levels.

I remember the conversation clearly, because it forced a decision I could no longer postpone.

Hein and I were talking about leadership capability, not in theory but in reality. The strategy was in place. The ambition was clear. What wasn't clear yet was whether our leadership bench could carry it.

I said what had been bothering me for weeks.

"Even if the strategy is right," I told him, "it won't work if leaders keep leading the way they always have."

He didn't hesitate.

"That's exactly the issue," Hein said. "This transformation isn't only asking people to do different things. It's asking them to behave as different leaders."

I nodded. "Not everyone will want that."

"Or be able to," he replied. "That doesn't make them bad leaders. It just means the model has changed." We both knew ING was full of strong, capable people who had succeeded in a very different environment: one based on hierarchy, control, and predictability. We were now asking for empowerment, ambiguity, and speed.

That shift was professional. It was also personal.

"What do we do?" I asked.

Hein was direct. "We have to help leaders figure out for themselves whether they actually belong in ING's next chapter."

I pushed back. "That sounds risky."

"It is," he said. "Pretending otherwise is worse. If someone isn't aligned, they'll slow everything down. Quietly. Respectfully. Decisively."

We sat with that for a moment.

I said, "I don't want this to become a training program."

Hein agreed. "Then it must be real. Same experience for everyone. No shortcuts."

"That will mean people leaving," I said.

"Yes," Hein said. "That's not failure. That's integrity."

The Think Forward Leadership Program (TFLP) was born that day. Many people leaned in fully. Others discovered ING's transformation wasn't theirs to lead.

Leading the transformation wasn't about convincing people to follow.

It was about creating the conditions for clarity and trusting people to decide.

TRANSFORMATION LIVES OR DIES WITH LEADERSHIP

Transformation does not succeed on strategy alone. It lives or dies with leadership. That is why it is a core element of the framework and why we invested so heavily in leadership development and leadership selection. As ING changed, the demands on leaders changed with it. We needed leaders who could empower others, make decisions in uncertainty, and model the behavior we were asking of the organization. This chapter explains why leadership mattered so deeply to the transformation, how we invested in developing it, and how we made deliberate choices about who could lead ING into its next chapter.

Leading the transformation required balancing two sides.

One side was about execution: how to run a large-scale change program.

- How do you set priorities?
- Who monitors progress?
- How do you escalate issues and resolve blockers quickly?

Execution, in the technical sense, is relatively straightforward. You can track progress on a dashboard. Red, yellow, green. You set clear OKRs and KPIs to measure progress.

You can measure KPIs, monitor delivery, and hold people accountable. Strategy doesn't live in a spreadsheet, however. If the culture doesn't support it, the strategy won't take hold, no matter how many speeches, memos, or town halls you give. Later in the transformation, focusing on global standardization, we relied on tools like the quarterly business reviews (QBRs) to zoom in on urgent matters and zoom out to assess whether we were staying on course. It meant managing technology, aligning priorities, and running a disciplined "war room" to drive delivery and accountability.

The other side focused on shaping leadership, talent, culture, capabilities, and performance management. This included changes to the top executive team, the creation of the Leadership Council, the TFLP, the Orange Code, and tools like the Organizational Health Index (OHI), which we'll explore later in the chapter. The OHI helped us track progress toward the leadership archetype we were building: one grounded in empowerment, collaboration, and capability.

It was the deeper challenge and one I couldn't solve alone. ING leadership had to evolve.

When we embarked on our transformation journey, we quickly realized that having a clear strategy and purpose was only the beginning. The strategy had taken shape over months of discussion. The real challenge was getting everyone aligned across more than forty countries, 1,000+ teams, and countless local nuances. We needed every manager not only to understand our new direction but to actively translate it into their own realities. If someone didn't believe in it, that was okay; there were other banks where they might feel more aligned. If they did believe in it, then they had a responsibility to help implement it. Together.

So, we needed to get the whole of ING on board, not only leadership. Alignment didn't happen behind closed doors, it happened on stage, in rooms full of people, through story and repetition. Every speech became an opportunity to connect the dots between our strategy and the culture required to bring it to life. We needed to created space for honest dialogue. Not just top-down presentations but real conversations. And I reinforced a simple but important message: "This isn't *my* strategy. It's *ours*. We developed it together."

That message became a constant theme, in every leadership keynote, every team meeting, every one-on-one.

- We needed to deliver on our customer promise.
- A seamless digital experience is nonnegotiable.
- Data analytics are essential for understanding our clients in a digital world.
- Innovation is critical to delight clients and stay ahead of the competition.

ALIGNING STRATEGY, LEADERSHIP, AND CULTURE

The first time I shared the Think Forward strategy with the top 200 was on March 29 and 30, 2014. As they had participated in developing it, I found it important to share the full story with them before we would inform the outside world a day later. It took place in Amsterdam, in an old industrial plant. We were in a room designed almost like a small stadium with two opposing sets of bleachers. I stood in the center, on the floor, not on a stage, so that no matter where someone sat, they couldn't escape the story. That was intentional. We didn't want a hierarchy between the speaker and the team. We wanted a connection.

As I moved through the room, I could feel the energy shift. Some people leaned in. Others drifted, half there, half somewhere else. That's normal, but many connected to the message, and those were who we built momentum with.

THE POWER OF VISUAL STORYTELLING

In those talks, I kept coming back to a few key themes:

- Purpose
- Customer experience
- Collaboration
- Standardization
- Innovation

I repeated them often. Not to sound rehearsed but to anchor the transformation in shared language. These were not abstract ideas; they were the cornerstones of the shift we were making. These were directly related to the outcome of the workstreams that many in the room had been part of.

The talks weren't about numbers. I never used them. Not once. I knew from experience: when you put a financial result or forecast on a slide, people stop listening and start questioning. They challenge the assumption, get pulled into the data, and the story gets lost.

Instead, I focused on narrative. On pace. On tone. On body language. Because most of what we communicate has nothing to do with the words themselves; it's *how* we say them. When people hear conviction in your voice, when they see you move with intention, they remember what you stand for.

Yes, I used visuals but not slides filled with bullet points or spreadsheets. The images behind me were simple. Visual cues that supported the emotion, not the math. Because humans don't remember lists; we remember feelings.

That was the point: to move people. To help them see themselves in the story and bring them along, not just intellectually but emotionally.

If storytelling helped connect hearts in the room, direct communication helped carry that connection across the organization. I didn't want those moments of clarity and conviction to stay confined to a stage or a single event. The question became how do you sustain that same authenticity when you're speaking to 54,000 people, not 200?

A NEW WAY TO COMMUNICATE

One of the most transformative tools we used to sustain authenticity was direct communication. For the first time, we had the means to reach every employee instantly, through short, self-recorded videos. No filters. No layers. Just me, speaking directly to our people.

Before that, we lived in a world of intranets. And while

intranets were once revolutionary, replacing printed news-
letters and enabling daily digital updates, they had become
overwhelming. Thousands of messages, too much noise. People
would log in, get lost, and miss what mattered.

So we made two changes.

First, every intranet homepage, regardless of region or country, had to open with the strategy front and center. That way,
every employee, every day, saw the same message. The hope
was simple: they'd pause and think, "Does my calendar reflect
this strategy? If not, what do I need to change?"

Second, we replaced formal CEO memos with short videos,
one to two minutes at most. Casual, candid, and to the point.
In simple language. In one-liners, if I could. Because this communication was about moving people to action, not sharing
what I thought.

If I was at Money20/20 for example, I'd share why I was
there: "This is where the future of finance is made, and I'm
here to share ING's story and how we manage our relationships
with fintechs."

These weren't daily, but they were regular and always intentional. We called them snackable updates. Simple. Human. Fast.

Most importantly, they let me bypass many layers of hierarchy and speak straight to 54,000 people at once. That created
energy. Not push but pull. When people feel seen and included,
they lean in. They feel that they belong and are part of making
the change.

TRUST AS THE STARTING POINT

It was one of those early conversations. The bank was still shak-
ing off the last years of survival. Everyone was tired. Everyone
was cautious.

Mark Buitenhek, ING's global head of transaction services at the time, was already at the office when I arrived.

We didn't start with vision. We started with reality.

"If you want my honest view, we're spending a lot of time protecting what we have. That's not where the real threat is coming from," Mark said.

That alone told me something. "You're thinking big tech."

He didn't hesitate. "Of course. They've already entered payments. We're still arguing country by country while they're building platforms."

That was the moment I knew we were speaking the same language.

Not because he agreed with me but because he had arrived there on his own.

Most people were still comparing ING to other banks. Mark wasn't. He was benchmarking us against technology companies, against ecosystems, against scale.

"What would you do differently?" I asked.

He leaned forward. "Stop thinking in branches. Stop thinking in acquisitions. If you want to enter a market like Germany in SME banking, you don't buy another bank. You build, or acquire, technology. You go mobile first. Platform first."

There was no pitch in his voice. No politics. Just clarity.

I'd heard a lot of smart ideas in my career. What stood out here wasn't novelty; it was coherence. His thinking already fit the direction we were moving toward.

"That will make people uncomfortable."

Mark smiled. Not defiantly. Matter of fact. "It already does."

We were aligned. From that point on, the pattern was simple.

I didn't need to convince Mark of the direction; I needed to remove friction so he could move.

When he pushed for centralizing payments (one platform,

all countries), I backed him. Not because it was easy but because it was inevitable.

When he said negotiating country by country made no sense, and that scale would unlock real value, I agreed. When the resistance came, as it always does, I stayed visible.

"If you need more time, take it. If you need more investment, we'll find it. We're building a platform, not chasing quarters," I told him.

He didn't abuse that trust. He used it.

The same thing happened with innovation. With Payconiq. With application programming interfaces (APIs). With agile in wholesale banking, where the resistance was fiercest.

Mark became an internal translator. Sometimes an irritant. Often an ambassador.

My trust in Mark was not accidental. I have always led from a simple premise: I trust people until they give me a reason not to. Trust, for me, is the starting point, not the reward at the end of the process. When you hire good people and give them clarity on direction and expectations, control adds very little value. Trust creates speed. It creates ownership. And it forces people to step up rather than wait to be told what to do. Of course, trust also comes with accountability. When that trust is broken, you act. But by leading with trust, you create an environment where people feel empowered to take responsibility, make decisions, and grow into the leadership the organization needs.

> "That outside-in, platform-driven way of thinking came together beautifully with the team. And because of that alignment, I had enormous support from Ralph for seven years. I could call him directly."
>
> —MARK BUITENHEK, FORMER ING GLOBAL HEAD OF TRANSACTION SERVICES

LEADING BY EXAMPLE

Communication and trust alone weren't enough. They had to be backed by action, by leadership that modeled the very behaviors and structures we were asking the organization to adopt.

We changed the executive team titles from "CEO of their division" to reflect their true role: first and foremost, as executive team members sharing overall responsibility, and second as heads (not CEO) of their respective functions or divisions. This was done to reinforce that we were a unified team focused on collaboration, not siloed executives.

We established KPIs that mixed executive team and individual metrics, covering strategy, risk management, culture, and commercial and financial performance. These top-level KPIs cascaded through the organization to ensure alignment. From the top of the pyramid all the way down to every colleague, consistently, recognizably, and measurably, we showed that everyone at ING played a vital role in delivering on our strategic priorities.

The executive team, soon joined by a COO, worked as one team to stay focused, agile, and fast in a dynamic world. We also made it a point to keep the executive team limited to seven members. If we believed in working in small, agile, multifunctional teams, we had to set the example ourselves.

In a later stage of the transformation, we balanced zooming out (seven-to-nine-year vision) with zooming in (three-month reviews and six-month plans) during the QBRs.

We also held quarterly sessions with the Leadership Council (see later in this chapter), our top leaders:

- Share progress
- Celebrate wins
- Address setbacks

- Create alignment
- Encourage learning from failure
- Reinforce empowerment and transparency

We reported to the Board of Directors every quarter, especially in the early stages.

Those efforts, from how we structured the executive team to how we managed execution and measured progress, were grounded in one essential principle: consistency. Because without consistency, none of it would stick.

CONSISTENCY AND TRANSFORMATION

> *"Ralph had long-term vision for the bank and remained completely consistent. That's the great thing about him. His thinking was utterly consistent. He never lost the plot."*
>
> —HEIN KNAAPEN, FORMER ING HEAD OF HR

The way we communicated, the tone, the cadence, the clarity, became a reflection of how we operated. At the heart of it all was consistency. That one principle shaped how we led, how we executed, and how we earned trust during the most difficult parts of the transformation.

The word I'm most often praised for is consistency. I'd hear, "You're so consistent."

I'd reply, "Of course I'm consistent. We've agreed on what we're going to do, so let's do it."

Sometimes people would show me something else. "This is *also* an opportunity."

I'd respond, "Yes, it's an opportunity, but that doesn't make it strategic. It's not a priority unless it aligns with our strategy. Otherwise, it's just a distraction." That's where consistency matters most.

Consistency and the discipline not to be distracted and to stay the course make people understand what fits and what doesn't. It is a very important element of successful transformation and needs to be exercised by the CEO: there is no escape!

THE IMPORTANCE OF A STRONG CULTURE: THE ORANGE CODE

It began with a simple premise. If we wanted to execute the Strategy on a Page through a high-performing organization, we needed to clearly define and support the behaviors that drive execution success. So we articulated three core behaviors we expected to see:

- Take it on and make things happen: We did not want people to wait for instruction if they knew what to do. We wanted them to act and own the outcome. This was the element of trust and empowerment.
- Help others to be successful: The way to build collaboration is expecting everyone to help others to be successful. Not yourself. Because if everyone helps each other, each will be successful.
- Always stay one step ahead: As the environment and customer expectations were changing quickly, we expected people to anticipate what's next and proactively manage risk.

We also developed these three core values:

- We're honest.
- We're prudent.
- We're responsible.

The Orange Code

Our behaviors

 **You take it on and make it happen**

 **You help others to be successful**

 **You are always a step ahead**

You take responsibility for getting it done, for keeping your promises, for the consequences of your actions.

You delegate to motivate others, maintain momentum, and create impact.

You ask actively for help and feedback. Your colleagues will help you succeed if you let them.

You speak up—crediting good work and having the courage to confront poor performance.

You collaborate—putting personal agendas aside to achieve the goals that matter to ING.

You listen—investing in others, irrespective of status, background, or opinion.

You contribute across business lines and bring in people from outside your area.

You trust the intention and expertise of others.

You challenge conventions, complexity and your own assumptions, but only when you are prepared to be part of the solution.

You bring change by adapting quickly when the situation calls for a new approach.

You invent and simplify—if it doesn't work, you reinvent it. If it does work, you make it better.

You are courageous—admitting and learning from mistakes by being open about them.

The Orange Code was born from intuition and values, not methodology. It was uncovering what people wanted and some already did by making it explicit and observable. Now we could also manage and coach expected behavior by making these an element of people's annual performance appraisals. We translated each individual's role and responsibility into clear, observable behaviors needed to do their job effectively. This was a crucial shift, enabling both individual development and disciplined execution. Without that alignment, consistent delivery on our customer and brand promise would not have been possible.

MEASURING EMPOWERMENT

Thus, the Orange Code didn't just describe the culture we aspired to; it gave us a concrete definition of empowered behavior.

Empowerment meant initiative, collaboration, and foresight. It meant creating an environment where people felt not only allowed but expected to step up. We knew values alone wouldn't change behavior. If we wanted to see empowerment in action, we had to track it.

So we measured it.

We implemented a quarterly pulse check, a recurring, structured way to listen to employees across the business. It helped us see whether empowerment was showing up in the day-to-day:

- Were people taking ownership?
- Did they feel trusted?
- Were they collaborating across silos?
- Where were we improving, and where were we falling short?

These pulse checks became an important way to manage progress in our transformation and became later a standard item in our QBRs.

THE KUDOS PROGRAM

One of the risks of any well-established framework is that it fades into the background. People still believe in it, but it no longer actively shapes behavior in the moment. That is where Kudos played a critical role promoting the Orange Code behavior and values.

Kudos was about attention, giving and receiving it. About pulling the Orange Code back into daily work in a way that felt human, timely, and authentic.

The premise was simple and supported by academic research: recognition reinforces behavior. Studies showed that compliments activate the same reward centers in the brain as financial incentives. Our own data confirmed something equally important: colleagues wanted to recognize one another but needed a clear, shared mechanism to do so.

To design that mechanism properly, we brought in an agency that specialized in developing games, not because we wanted to turn culture into entertainment but because they understood motivation, participation, and human behavior at scale. Together, we created a playful system that encouraged action without trivializing it and could be accessed through a digital tool on a mobile device or desktop application.

One design choice was intentional: the system rewarded giving Kudos more than receiving them. The point was not to accumulate recognition but to build a habit of noticing and reinforcing the right behaviors and values in others. By linking short, specific messages of appreciation directly to the Orange Code, and by limiting how many each person could give, the Kudos Program kept recognition intentional rather than performative.

This way, the Orange Code stayed present in daily interactions without feeling imposed.

BUILD TEAMS THROUGH UNDERSTANDING

Throughout my career, I've also used a technique called Management Drives to identify complementary strengths and put teams together. It's based on Graves's theory and uses the most intriguing assessment tool I've ever seen, only twenty questions that generate a color pattern of your thinking, logic, and how you act.

For people to understand themselves as a team, and for team

leaders to understand their teams, you must understand the logic, how you think, but also how you act in a daily context. For example, if I give you an assignment to go and get ten new clients, some people will say, "Okay," and just go, which is indicated through a red color. Others will say, "Well, if we have to get ten clients, let me make a plan," which is blue. Still others will think, *Let me consider how I do that*, which is yellow. And some will say, "Ten clients within a week? I can't do this by myself. I have to find a team to work with," which is green.

The key insight is that if you're a leader and you're very procedural, you generally have the tendency to look for people who are also very procedural because you think, *Well, if this approach works for me, then people who think the same way must be good, too.* That's exactly what you shouldn't do. That's why I'm a big diversity thinker.

Management Drives, apart from ethnic diversity and gender diversity, gives you a more objective perspective on how to bring diversity to the table, specifically regarding how people think, how they work, what their strengths are, and how you can motivate them.

That's why I've always prioritized diversity of thought and action, not just in how teams are built but in how they're led.

VALUING DIVERSE LEADERSHIP STYLES

I've always valued diversity on my team. I want people who challenge me, not clones. I hire for excellence, not similarity.

If someone operates with honesty, directness, and integrity, I'm open to whatever style they bring, emotional or rational, customer- or return-focused. I want my team to fill in my gaps.

Many companies suffer from leadership echo chambers. I work actively against that.

I know I'm not the smartest person in the room on every topic. That's not weakness; that's awareness. Some leaders lead with ego. I lead through empowerment and connection.

—MARK MILDERS, FORMER ING HEAD OF INVESTOR RELATIONS

Leading a strategy team is different from leading a retail organization. Investment bankers are more homogenous, rational, numbers driven. Retail banks are made up of marketers, product managers, and software engineers, but also of customer service reps, branch staff, phone agents, and people in different roles and locations who work nine to five.

All matter just as much. The key is meeting them where they are and speaking their different languages.

We can't expect front-line staff to care about return on equity like we do. That's not their strength. Their strength is in human connection, serving customers, building trust. That's what they're great at.

Our job as leaders is to recognize that and make sure they feel seen and supported for it.

Even with a strong, diverse leadership team, transformation brings a deeper reckoning, one that goes beyond diversity of styles, background, and experience and into personal alignment and commitment. That's where purpose came in.

Purpose thinking became the catalyst for everything, and early on, we recognized a major disconnect in how our leadership was structured.

Since we were essentially starting from scratch, though building on our history and DNA, and landed on empowerment as our core purpose, we realized we also had to empower our leaders in a completely different way.

This led us to a fundamental question: how do we make sure these leaders feel connected to the central purpose while also embracing a new way of management? We wanted leaders who would give direction and inspire people but ultimately ensure consistency across the organization. We had joint KPIs and cascaded them consistently to support execution, but we knew we needed to do more.

FROM 200 TO 50

To make that shift real, we had to start by rethinking who was at the table and whether our leadership structure truly reflected the organization we were trying to become.

When I took the lead at ING, I inherited its Management Council, a group of 200 of the bank's most senior ranking executives.

For many, the Management Council, as the top 200 was then called, had become a career milestone. People worked toward being part of it, an invitation to Management Council was like a promotion. A sign one had "made it." Each year, those invited would attend an annual strategy session where the CEO presented ING's state of the union: what we had done, how we had performed, and what they expected in the year ahead. It was an exclusive space people aspired to join.

The council was heavily weighted toward head-office functions, HR, finance, legal, risk, operations, and technology. While those roles were important, they didn't always reflect the day-to-day experience of our clients.

The voices we needed more of, the people closest to the customer, were underrepresented.

That wasn't the model we wanted going forward. We didn't want managers. We wanted leaders, people in charge of critical elements of our strategy, not people selected based on title or tenure.

So we made a bold move that shocked everyone: we presented the *Leadership* Council, a group of fifty, give or take, who would work with us quarterly, rather than annually. These fifty leaders wouldn't be chosen for their seniority or position but for the role they played and the impact they could have on developing and executing our strategy.

We still included key functional leaders but not in disproportionate numbers. We needed balance, because putting the customer at the center wasn't just a strategic imperative, it was our purpose. If we wanted to deliver on that promise, including the risk management around it, we had to make sure our leadership reflected the people doing the work.

We also added a few emerging talents to the mix. I'm not sure how consistently we applied it, but in some council meetings, we invited three or four younger professionals without formal leadership roles, people who could challenge us, keep us honest, and inject fresh perspectives. They were there to say things like, "You may think you're doing great, but here's where we're missing the mark" or "We should be moving faster."

We reshaped the new Leadership Council to better reflect the business. We elevated more business leaders, those on the front lines of client relationships, the ones who truly understood customer needs and market dynamics. Country managers remained central, but they were now joined by their marketing leads, wholesale banking heads, and others who could bring in the client perspective directly.

This shift in representation sent a clear signal: the transformation would not be led from behind a desk. It would be driven by those who understood the customer best and who were ready to lead in a new way.

THE SYMBOLIC POWER OF CHANGE

We also announced that it would replace the Management Council.

Of course, this shift meant disappointing many people, a massive risk. I explained the Leadership Council was different. This wasn't a demotion; it was a new model. Selection was based on the task at hand and on merit, not hierarchy. I made it clear the fifty weren't fixed, every year we would review the roster based on evolving priorities, and we did. Some people would rotate out, others would be invited in. It was not about status. It was about shared responsibility for implementation, follow-through, and solving the challenges ahead.

I did not want it to become a group that provided status but a group that collectively felt responsible for the implementation of the strategy at that phase. For the first phase (decentral implementation, 2014–2016), we had more country representation. For the second phase with more cross-border standardization (2017–2020), we added more tech and risk management representatives. Still, it wasn't an easy message for those who suddenly found themselves outside the inner circle. Imagine working at ING for twenty years, having made it into the Management Council and feeling rightfully proud, only to be told that while you were still a valued manager, you were not going to be part of the smaller group I'd be working with more regularly.

Those I sensed might take it personally, I called directly. I wanted them to understand that this wasn't a judgment on their past contributions or leadership; it also didn't mean they'd never be on the Leadership Council. Future priorities might require their expertise in the Leadership Council again. The Leadership Council's composition changed with the need for leaders with specific approaches and responsibilities.

Now the focus was on contribution, not hierarchy. It wasn't about status; it was about responsibility. The reshuffle had symbolic weight.

LEADERSHIP MANIFESTO

The first meeting of the new Leadership Council (January 2015) made the shift immediately clear: things were going to be different. Some were still surprised there were only fifty people in the room, but that was the point. This wasn't business as usual. This was a new way of leading. In a group of 200, you can hide, but in a group of fifty, you must take joint responsibility or speak up.

We spent two full days defining a shared code of working, our standards for how we'd operate together. We asked fundamental questions:

- What brings us together?
- What do we expect from each other?
- What kind of leaders do we need to be for this transformation to succeed?

The result was a document we called the Leadership Manifesto.

I didn't write it; they did. I empowered the group to develop the manifesto themselves: to articulate how they would make this happen and take this leadership forward, translate the strategy into their own environments, challenge one another, keep each other honest, and speak outside the sessions with one voice. It was essential that we communicated with respect but also in a way that was open and constructively challenging.

I told them, "You're going to write your own rules. If I write them, you'll just tell me why they're wrong, and I don't want that. I want you to lead. I'm empowering you to do this, but it must come from you. Then I'll review and give feedback."

That approach made all the difference. Because they wrote it, they owned it.

This moment in our transformation is still vivid for me. It was a massive change, one that would later prove essential when we rolled out our agile way of working. The signal we sent was loud and clear: leadership wasn't about seniority anymore. It was about values. It wasn't about who had been around the longest or who held the highest title; it was about who could contribute meaningfully to the transformation.

Speaking up because of your expertise and experience, not your rank or tenure. That alone represented a major cultural shift. To make the transformation work, we needed people who could collaborate across silos, take initiative when needed, and step into ownership, not because they were told to but because they saw it as their responsibility.

All of this was about more than just structure. It was about creating a new kind of leadership culture, one rooted in contribution, collaboration, and courage.

SHARING MY CRUCIBLES WITH THE LEADERSHIP COUNCIL

The first time the Leadership Council came together, we organized a dinner at a restaurant in Amsterdam. It was an intentional choice. The group was much smaller than what we were used to, and we were asking something fundamentally different of one another. We were going to implement the purpose and the broader Think Forward strategy together. That required trust across a group larger than a typical executive team.

It was imperative for this group to know and trust each other personally, as we had quite a few challenges ahead of us, and we needed to rely on each other.

Most people knew each other, but many had grown up in different geographies, functions, or businesses within ING. They had rarely worked closely together and did not yet know one another well enough to be truly open. That changed that evening.

As part of the evening, we did an exercise around people's strengths, talent, and purpose. Although we had not started the TFLP yet, when personal purpose was to be defined, during the dinner I got up and shared the defining challenges of my career.

After the first course, I stood up and asked for everyone's attention. I began by telling my own story: where I grew up, about my family, and the values that mattered most to me. But I went a step further. I shared a few crucibles: experiences that had shaped who I am, how I think, and how I behave as a leader.

Early in my career, I was fortunate to have several senior mentors. One of them became the risk manager for ING's international banking business and invited me to join his division. One day, while we were discussing an acquisition loan that required approval, his phone rang. There was an urgent request to approve a trade in the dealing room. The call was on speaker, and I listened as arguments went back and forth. In the end, he decided not to approve the trade, much to the disappointment of the other side.

A few days later, the market turned sharply. A significant trading loss emerged, and ING had to disclose it publicly. As risk manager, he was held responsible and immediately removed from his role by the board. Weeks later, it became clear that a board member had overruled his original decision and approved the trade, but the damage had already been done. My mentor's reputation had suffered, the trust between him and the board was irreparably broken, and a very talented banker's career took a turn, without him being at fault.

Being so close to those events had a lasting impact on me. It fundamentally shaped how I thought about careers and leadership. I became far less fearful of what the future might bring and deeply convinced that the only sensible approach is to do your very best and remain true to your values. If that is not enough, or if circumstances beyond your control intervene, so be it. That experience made me more independent in my thinking and less politically driven. You cannot plan your career in detail; you can only make sure you enjoy what you do and stand by who you are.

Later on in my career, I was asked to move to Bucharest to lead ING Bank Romania. It was mid-1999, and the country's economy was in poor shape. Inflation ran between 45 and 55 percent, and central bank interest rates were often above 80 percent. ING was performing well, supported by a group of young, talented bankers navigating these challenges alongside their clients.

I had no experience operating in such an environment. I also had no real management experience, yet from day one I was responsible for a team of 150 to 200 people. During the transition, my predecessor informed me that he was joining a competitor and that he was attempting to take several members of the management team with him.

Faced with this, I called the leader who had asked me to take on the role. I said, "You've sent me to a country I don't know, with a culture and language that are new to me, into an unstable economic environment, running banking activities I have no experience in, managing a large group of people for the first time in my career…and now the management team is falling apart. What made you think I was the right person for this?"

He replied simply, "I've seen how you act in uncertain situations in risk management, and I'm convinced you can do this." And then he hung up.

I had never felt as lonely as I did in that moment. But I also had a leader who dared to empower me, someone who believed in my potential more than I did myself. That experience taught me that trust and empowerment are not only powerful tools in delegation but also a profound source of motivation.

Setting the example that evening, opening up this way, lead to everyone in the room sharing their crucibles at the tables they were seated. Some amazing life stories were shared, creating understanding and massive respect for one another. Another crucial step in creating a top leadership team was taken. During the personal purpose exercise we all did later, I eventually articulated my personal purpose as "I rock your world today, to go where you haven't gone before." What I've always tried to do, what I did at ING, is motivate people to do things they didn't think they could or had the potential or talent to do. That's what our transformation was about: ambitious, aspirational, and compelling. It pushed people to develop their talent beyond what they thought was possible.

THE PERSONAL PURPOSE EXERCISE

> "When you're connected to your purpose, everything you do generates energy, even the hard work. But when you drift too far from it for too long, you end up depleted, burned out, and questioning everything. Purpose is the fuel that makes leadership sustainable."
>
> —NICK CRAIG, AUTHOR OF *LEADING WITH PURPOSE*

Banking is a traditional industry. When I was CEO, many people at ING believed things should stay the same. Some had built their careers in a world of hierarchy, predictability, and control, and suddenly, they were being asked to work in a completely new way.

That kind of shift doesn't just change structures. It tests identities.

I had to let go of people I liked, good leaders who had contributed a lot to the company but who couldn't or wouldn't adapt. Some didn't buy into the new direction. Others believed in it but didn't feel comfortable or capable of operating in the new model. They stepped away on their own.

To help people navigate that decision, we introduced a personal purpose exercise. Over the course of three days, each leader explored their own formative experiences, core values, and sources of energy, ultimately articulating a personal purpose statement. Then, they compared that purpose to ING's.

If the alignment was strong, the transformation felt energizing. If there was a disconnect, people felt it immediately. That misalignment didn't make them bad leaders; it just meant they might not thrive in this next chapter for ING. Trying to force it would only lead to frustration or burnout. Quite a few leaders came to that realization themselves. They looked inward and said, "This isn't my shop anymore."

That was okay. Because when someone's personal purpose no longer fits the organization's direction, the most respectful outcome is clarity, for them and for the company.

THINK FORWARD LEADERSHIP PROGRAM

We also did the personal purpose work as an executive team so we could lead by example and truly understand what would come from it. Each member went through the same reflective exercise: exploring their personal purpose.

- What shaped me?
- What gives me energy?
- Where are my talents?
- What does balance look like for me?

After we saw how powerful the personal purpose work had been for us, how it helped us better understand our strengths, our energy sources, and how each could contribute more meaningfully to ING, we decided to expand the effort.

That's when we launched the TFLP.

Every leader, whether new to ING or already in place, went through the TFLP.

The program began with a deep understanding of our purpose and strategy, but it didn't stop there. Each participant was asked to define their own purpose, what drives them, where they create value, and how that personal purpose could align with ING's transformation.

From there, we asked people to map their ambitions in reverse: what they wanted to accomplish five years from now, three years out, two years, six months, three months, two months, one month. It was a structured process for connecting long-term vision to near-term action, grounding strategy in personal accountability.

Over time, the program reached nearly 5,000 leaders across the organization. Everyone went through the same experience. This wasn't incremental training; it was designed to spark a step change in mindset and behavior. We talked about 10x thinking, not 10 percent improvements. About challenging the status quo, not preserving it.

The message was clear: we were choosing talent over tenure, merit over hierarchy, and contribution over comfort. It wasn't easy, and it certainly wasn't conventional, but it was necessary for the kind of transformation we were driving.

The TFLP was very successful.

A GIFT OF SELF-DISCOVERY

It might sound strange to say a training is successful when some participants decide to leave afterward. I think it's pretty cool for a company to help someone uncover what truly drives them and then support their decision if they realize they're not in the right place to fulfill that purpose. That's not failure. That's integrity.

In fact, it may be the greatest gift we could give them. Being let go without that self-awareness, after years of service, loyalty, and effort, can be devastating. When someone comes to that realization on their own terms however, it's a blessing.

When you've been in a role for a while, when peer pressure, status, or financial rewards become deeply intertwined with your lifestyle, it can be hard to let go. Those things alone shouldn't define you, though. Rediscovering your purpose helps you see that clearly.

That was a vital part of the leadership journey for every leader at ING.

SPENCER STUART'S LEADERSHIP ASSESSMENT

After the personal purpose exercise, the next piece of our leadership development approach was creating a consistent, integrated way to assess both talent and potential. For this, we used two primary tools, one of which was a formal assessment process led by Spencer Stuart.

Everyone in senior leadership, including me, underwent these evaluations. The goal was simple: to measure whether we were demonstrating the behaviors we said we valued.

Because I can preach empowerment, collaboration, and forward-thinking all day, but if I don't embody those behaviors, I won't earn followership.

Empowerment isn't about being "nice." It's about clarity and accountability. We clearly defined expectations per role and connected them to our strategy, through activating the Orange Code, as mentioned earlier. We coached leaders on what empowerment really meant in their role and ensured our governance structure closed gray areas where ownership might fall through.

These assessments weren't just top-down. They included input from peers, reports, and people further down the organization. It was a 360-degree view of how each leader showed up.

I remember one insight from my own assessment that stuck with me:

I'm naturally a forward thinker, but I tend to open up once I've already decided where I'm headed. The feedback was that I needed to bring others into my thinking earlier, to co-shape the path forward, not just share the destination.

That was powerful. And it wasn't just about me. This was how we assessed most of our leadership team, not just where they were but where they could grow and how we could help them get there. It gave us a shared lens for development and made leadership growth a core part of the transformation, not a side effort.

The real test, however, was whether the development of our leadership, establishing their personal purpose, the assessment of their growth areas would cascade through the entire organization, whether employees at every level could feel the difference in how we worked, communicated, and made decisions.

To know if the culture was truly shifting, we needed a way to measure it.

MEASURING ORGANIZATIONAL HEALTH AND LEADERSHIP DEVELOPMENT

Throughout the transformation, as we implemented changes, one of our core concerns was ensuring that we acted consistently with the kind of organization we aspired to become. The OHI helped us do that. It provided a structured way to measure how people experienced the company across nine dimensions that reflect different leadership and cultural archetypes.

Depending on how you score on those dimensions, you might lean toward one of the seven defined archetypes. For example, a command-and-control model, execution-oriented and highly effective in manufacturing, would be exemplified by Toyota. Or a leadership-driven model, where direction, motivation, and vision are core strengths. Tesla is often seen this way.

There's no right or wrong archetype; each is a legitimate way to manage. If we wanted to become a truly empowered, agile, and customer-driven organization, we had to evolve toward a very specific archetype.

So we used the OHI to track that evolution, and we used the Market Focus archetype as our model. (Amazon is often cited as an example.) Over time, we analyzed the extent to which we were moving toward that archetype.

Were we moving in the right direction? Were people experiencing the shift, not just in structure but in how we worked together, made decisions, and led?

The results helped us zero in on the areas that mattered most. In total, the OHI looked at twenty-nine management practices. From those, we identified the top five that would be most critical to our success, nearly all of which aligned with empowerment, collaboration, and expertise-based leadership rather than, for example, hierarchy.

Even with the right behaviors in place, the values and behaviors we codified in the Orange Code, we had to ask a deeper question: do our people have the capabilities to operate this way?

In many cases, the answer was no.

This came through, for example, in technology. We had too many project managers and not enough software engineers. It wasn't just tech. Across the organization, we saw capability gaps, places where people had the right mindset but not the right tools or expertise to thrive in the new model.

That insight also came from the OHI. It revealed cultural and capability gaps and helped us understand where we needed to build, hire, and invest in capability. To sustain the transformation, we couldn't just change behavior; we had to upgrade skills...and we had to do it deliberately.

Different practices are separately measured on how they contribute to these outcomes and drive organizational health

Outcomes

Practices

Direction
- Shared vision
- Employee involvement
- Strategic clarity

Leadership
- Supportive
- Consultative
- Challenging
- Authoritative

Culture and climate
- Open and trusting
- Creative and entrepreneurial
- Internally competitive
- Operationally disciplined

Accountability
- Personal ownership
- Role clarity
- Performance contracts
- Consequence management

Coordination and control
- Financial management
- Professional standards
- Risk management
- People performance review
- Operational management

Capabilities
- Talent acquisition
- Talent development
- Process based
- Outsourced leadership

Motivation
- Open and meaningful value
- Inspirational leaders
- Career opportunities
- Financial incentives
- Rewards and recognition

Innovation and learning
- Top-down innovation
- Bottom-up innovation
- Knowledge sharing
- Capturing external ideas

External orientation
- Government and community relations
- Competitive insights
- Customer focus
- Business partnerships

The Organizational Health Index characterizes health in terms of specific outcomes.

However, it separately measures the practices that contribute to these outcomes, and hence examines the real drivers of health.

In addition to working on culture and capabilities, we introduced a new, very different approach to setting targets and evaluating performance in 2016.

Performance management is the spine of company performance. It is where strategy and annual plans translate into individual priorities and where ambition either accelerates or quietly stalls. If we wanted our strategy and culture to show up in daily behavior, performance management had to change.

We distinguished between job expectations, stretch ambitions, and the Orange Code. Within the stretch ambitions, we shifted to a 50/50 weighting between financial and nonfinancial business ambitions.

The nonfinancial side included strategic priorities such as NPS, primary customer growth, and improvements in compliance, operational, and financial risk management. We also evaluated performance based on behaviors and values that aligned with the Orange Code.

I wanted to be appraised using the same approach by the ING Supervisory Board, setting an example that strategy, culture, and behavior mattered just as much as commercial and financial success.

We also recognized that performance management is not a once-a-year exercise. It requires continuous interaction between employees and their managers: clear expectations, frequent feedback, and honest conversations about progress and development. That shift demanded new skills from managers at all levels, and we invested deliberately in building their confidence and capability to lead those conversations well.

We went further with the introduction of Step Up Performance Management. In the financial industry, variable compensation is often tied to annual targets, which can lead to conservative goal setting. Leaders may deliberately underestimate what they can achieve to ensure they hit their KPIs.

We came to understand that effective performance management depends first and foremost on the skills, and therefore the confidence, of managers to engage in ongoing, constructive performance conversations with their teams.

A critical change was moving away from purely numerical ratings toward more descriptive performance assessments. This shifted the focus from scoring to dialogue. Ratings now had to be explained, not just assigned. For example, when a colleague received an "Improvement Required" assessment, managers were expected to clearly articulate why, identify specific areas for development, and outline how improvement could be supported through learning, coaching, or new experiences. This fundamentally changed the quality of the conversation.

Step Up Performance was designed to promote and deliver on that change in mindset. We encouraged leaders to be more aspirational or move faster, but we also ensured their performance would be assessed in light of that ambition. In this model, whether for a financial or nonfinancial target, a colleague delivering 90 percent of an aspirational target could receive a stronger appraisal than someone delivering 110 percent of a safe one. This ensured alignment not just around what we achieved but how we pursued it, for everyone, reinforcing the behaviors and momentum we needed for change.

THE PUSH AND PULL DYNAMIC

Many things were happening at the same time: trainings, personal development, Leadership Council meetings, town halls, keynotes, global travel. That was intentional. We weren't waiting for one piece to be finished before starting the next.

The transformation had to move in parallel. Real change isn't linear; it's a flywheel. Every turn, every touchpoint, added momentum.

Not everyone moved at the same pace. Some middle managers felt left behind. Others resisted quietly, uncomfortable with what the changes meant for their role or influence. Even then, we knew we had to keep them engaged…and we did it two ways: by communicating clearly from the top and connecting directly with the people they managed.

When I stood in front of frontline teams, branch staff, software engineers, marketers, I didn't just share strategy and what we were doing. I listened. I translated. I tried to make the story real for them, and something powerful happened. The energy we created at the edges started pushing inward. People began to say, "We believe in this story. We want to be part of this. What are we doing to move faster?"

That pull from below created a dynamic tension. Change was no longer something being imposed from above. It was something being demanded from below. Even those unsure about the direction found themselves swept up in it because when your own teams start leaning into a new future, you can't sit back and resist. You must move.

That's how transformation sticks, not just through structure, leadership, or speeches but through energy. Top-down and bottom-up, moving together.

Leading the transformation at ING was never just about installing new systems or renaming teams. It was about rewiring how we thought, led, and worked together, top to bottom, inside and out. We aligned strategy with culture, leadership with purpose, and talent with contribution, like the framework explains. We connected the dots consistently and continuously. We gave people the tools to evolve, the space to reflect, and the clarity to opt in, or opt out, with integrity. That's what made the transformation sustainable. Not just because we changed the rules but because we changed the players, the playbook, and the very spirit of the game.

BECOMING A TALENT MAGNET

When I became CEO, ING was still carrying the reputational weight of the 2008 financial crisis. People questioned whether it was a place worth working for. Also, discussions around strict remuneration for bankers in the Netherlands did not help in attracting talent that was sensitive to this.

ING's Think Forward strategy transformed us from a financial conglomerate emerging from restructuring (at a time when many colleagues were uncertain about their jobs and cost control was essential for survival) into something truly distinctive.

The strategy, and the way we implemented it, created a powerful employee brand. We were not a pure tech company, but we were also no longer a slow-moving incumbent. We were a first mover: client-first and digital-first. In many countries, we operated as a genuine challenger, with a neobank mindset, and that required a different kind of talent. People who might have once set their sights on companies like Google were now drawn to ING because of our mission.

We needed strong engineers, leaders who were comfortable with empowerment, creative digital designers, and platform thinkers. These people do not join a company for a traditional banking reward system of variable pay and perks alone. They join organizations that live their purpose, that are committed to sustainability, and that offer a compelling story in which individuals can see their role...and how they can make a visible difference.

The Talent Magnet Flywheel

How organizations build and sustain competitive advantage through self-reinforcing excellence

8
Visible Success
Proof of winning in commercial growth (number of customers), financial growth (revenues, profit, EBITDA margin), and sustainability (linked to Sustainable Development Goals)

1
Clear Purpose
A compelling reason for being that provides meaning, direction, and confidence in the future

Chapter 3: The Power of Purpose

2
Strategic Ambition
Customer-centric story people want to join—inviting them to help build something better

Chapter 2: The Sun Rises Orange

7
Inspiring Campus
Physical environment designed for collaboration, learning, and energy that attracts and retains talent

Chapter 8: ING's Campus

Talent Magnet
Self-reinforcing system of attraction and retention

3
Sustainability Impact
Serious long-term commitments that signal responsibility and values resonating with talent

Chapter 10: Impact at Scale

6
Career Investment
Deliberate focus on skill development and clear growth pathways for ambitious professionals

5
Modern Working
Progressive collaboration models and practices that top talent expects and thrives in

Chapter 7: The New Way of Working

4
Technology Edge
Digital capabilities as differentiator enabling innovation, speed, and modern ways of working

Chapter 6: The Blueprint of a Digital Bank

They also look for places where technology is not treated as a cost but as a way of doing business differently; where there are real proof points in user experience and innovation; where the head office feels like a campus, with open spaces and a look and feel that signals care for how people spend a large part of their working lives.

That shift didn't just support our strategy; it accelerated it. We began attracting people with different profiles: more innovative thinkers, more digitally fluent talent, more talented engineers, better bankers, more people who would never have considered joining a traditional bank before. That influx of fresh perspectives helped catalyze cultural change from within. Transformation wasn't only driven by the people already inside; it was accelerated by the energy and ideas of those coming in.

THE TALENT MAGNET FLYWHEEL

This flywheel shows how organizations become (and remain) a talent magnet by designing a system where each element reinforces the next and momentum compounds over time.

It starts with purpose: a clear reason for being that gives people meaning, direction, and confidence in where the organization is going. Purpose is translated into a compelling story, a strategic ambition people want to join for, with customers at the core (Chapter 5) and a mindset that invites individuals to help build something better.

That story is made credible through serious sustainability commitments (Chapter 10: Impact at Scale), signaling long-term responsibility and values that resonate deeply with current and future talent. With trust established, technology becomes a differentiator (Chapter 6: The Blueprint of a Digital Bank), not just a tool, enabling innovation, speed, and modern ways of working (Chapter 7: The New Way of Working) that top talent expects.

The organization then deliberately invests in careers, offering clear skill development and a working environment designed for collaboration, learning, and energy, embodied in the campus (Chapter 8: ING's Campus). This attracts and retains high-caliber people who want to grow, not just work.

Also, of course, people want to be part of a winning team. Our rapid growth in digital-primary customers and our industry-leading financial results provided that final proof point.

These outcomes validate the story and increase the organization's attractiveness to talent even further. As each loop turns, the flywheel accelerates: drawing in more talent, strengthening performance, and making the organization increasingly hard to compete with or imitate. Together, these elements made ING a magnet for talent in the years from 2014 to 2020.

ORANGE BLOOD

ING has always had a strong culture, one of self-starting, values-driven people who take initiative and do the right thing. It feels like a family, spanning countries and time zones. It's hard to describe but easy to recognize once you've experienced it. We call it "orange blood" running through our veins.

Even colleagues from businesses that were sold during the restructuring (or those who decided to leave) still refer to that feeling with pride. Once you have orange blood in your veins, you always will. That same sense of identity extended to the executive team as well.

ING has long been a magnet for talented people, in part because of our culture of accelerating talent development through trust and empowerment. I'm a product of that system myself. Across the many leadership roles I held at ING, I was consistently supported by good people, and that was especially true during my time as CEO.

I'm particularly proud that those who left the top team during my tenure and, even afterward, went on to secure high-level roles elsewhere. I'm proudest of all that the Supervisory Board was able to find my successor from within the executive team itself.

We had reshaped our leadership, clarified our behaviors, and rebuilt our internal spine. Transformation, however, exists to serve the customer.

CHAPTER 5

CUSTOMER AT THE CORE

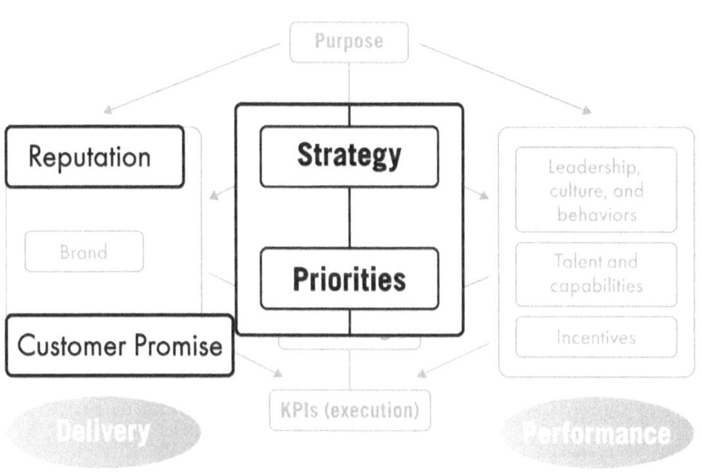

I didn't start by asking how we could build a better app.

I started by asking a simpler, more uncomfortable question: *do we know our customers anymore?*

That question had been sitting quietly inside ING for years. For some parts of the bank, especially those who had lived through ING Direct in its early days, the answer was painfully obvious. We had once been obsessed with the customer. Then the crisis came, and survival took over. Cost, capital, compliance, returns. Somewhere along the way, customer centricity became something we talked about rather than something we practiced.

I remember one moment that crystallized this for me.

Ignacio Juliá Vilar, ING Poland's Head of Retail Banking Segment at the time, was asked to lead one of the workstreams on customer experience. He presented the findings of his workstream to the top 200 during the first weekend when I took over. Instead of talking about products or channels, he told a story. He talked about a young woman named Ana. Her age. Her family. Her first job. Her ambitions. As he spoke, someone illustrated her life in real time beside him.

And then he stopped and asked the room a hard question: "Do we really know Ana?"

Ana, he reminded them, was one of our customers. Yet, despite selling her savings products and investments, we had no real understanding of who she was, what she needed, or what mattered to her. We were organized around products and distribution, not customers or understanding their needs.

That was the moment the conversation shifted.

We needed to become a customer-centric company again.

That insight became foundational to how we rebuilt ING. It shaped our strategy, our operating model, our culture, and the way we talked about ourselves, inside the bank and out. If we couldn't understand Ana, how could we claim to be relevant in her life? Relevance, more than scale or size, would define whether we had a future at all.

Customer at the core wasn't a slogan; it was a return to who we were when we were at our best.

CONNECTED TO THE PEOPLE WE SERVE

Throughout my entire career, I never stopped meeting with customers. As CEO of ING, I made it a point to stay personally connected to the people we served. Every week, I saw at least three to four clients.

I also maintained direct relationships with several customers I'd picked up early in my career. People sometimes asked why I kept those relationships. The answer was simple: I had been there from the beginning, and I didn't see a reason to step away just because my title had changed.

One of them dated all the way back to 2003. Even after I became CEO, I continued to be the principal relationship manager for that company. It was a fast-growing industrial company in the Netherlands, led by an entrepreneur with a powerful mission, to keep industrial jobs in the country. We developed a strong working relationship, but that didn't mean I always said yes. On the contrary, we sometimes did not agree or felt that elements of the business were risky. By being open and working to understand each other, we built real trust.

Later, when I transitioned to a different role in wholesale banking, I was expected to no longer manage Dutch clients. Then I moved to become the CEO of ING Belgium. Of course, I developed some good relationships for ING in those roles, but I *also* kept a few Dutch relationships.

I stayed in touch with the company even after I left ING. I cared for the business and the family. He passed away suddenly, and one of his children took over the business: same name, same spirit. The relationship continued.

From my first day in banking to my last day in the office, I managed my own client relationships. That was never a chore; it was who I was. Being close to the customer wasn't a leadership tactic or strategic pillar. For me, it was the most natural thing in the world. It grounded everything I did and reminded me, always, who we were doing it for.

ING redefined itself around a single, animating belief, that the customer must always be at the center, and how that belief shaped our strategy, culture, and digital innovation. That's the role customer promise plays in the framework.

SHIFTING TO A CUSTOMER-CENTRIC STRATEGY

"When it comes to digital transformation, banks have very similar plans. The difference is in the execution. It's all about the people and culture and how you get more than 50,000 people working together effectively. It starts with strong leadership...It is about mobilizing people...making them individually and collectively accountable to become sincerely, truly, and obsessively customer-centric."

—BENOÎT LEGRAND, FORMER ING CHIEF INNOVATION OFFICER

"It's not about us. It's about you."

That simple phrase became more than a mantra; it captured the essence of our transformation. As we shifted from a product-centric to a customer-first strategy, we weren't interested in generic taglines like "for a better future" or "we help you save." This wasn't about marketing. It was about redefining the bank's role in people's or companies' lives.

We wanted to empower customers to move forward, to stay a step ahead in life and business, without getting in their way. I used to describe it as being invisible yet indispensable. Someone once called it "wallpaper," something that holds a room together without drawing attention.

To me, however, it went deeper than that.

Our role wasn't to be at the center of the customer's story. It was to enable their story quietly, reliably, and intuitively. To be ever-present in the background, ensuring things work without inserting ourselves into the spotlight.

That's the paradox of a truly great financial experience: the better we are at serving our customers, the less they should notice us. In that quiet, frictionless presence, we deliver the very essence of what a modern bank should be.

That sense of pride and quiet determination shaped how we approached the rebuilding process. It was never theoretical. I had spent my entire career working directly with customers, and I carried that with me into every role, including CEO.

That perspective helped anchor our transformation in something real, because if we were going to prove who we were, we had to start by remembering who we served.

THE STRIKING DISCONNECT

Before 2008, ING Direct had already earned a reputation as the "non-bank." It entered rigid, siloed retail banking markets, starting in Canada, with a fundamentally different model. Most retail banks at the time were distant from their customers, both in mindset and structure. ING Direct had flipped that. We were seen as a true customer champion.

ING Direct stood out because it was simple, direct, and deeply customer centric. It consistently achieved the highest customer satisfaction and NPSs in the market. That was true well before the crisis. We weren't just saying "customer first." We were doing it.

Then came 2008. Every negative stereotype about banking, especially the idea that banks had lost touch with their customers, was amplified in the media and public discourse.

In the Netherlands, as ING received aid from the Dutch State, that sentiment hit particularly hard. Even though ING Direct had been viewed as a refreshing alternative in many international markets, in our home country, we were lumped in with the rest of the industry.

That disconnect was striking. Globally, ING was seen as not a traditional bank. We were an outlier, a challenger brand with customer loyalty to match. But at home, we became a focal point for public anger. That contradiction shaped how we approached the recovery.

We needed to go back to our strength of putting the customer at the center and be a challenger at the forefront of change for our clients. We lost some of that because during the crisis, our energy was consumed by survival, not innovation.

A RENEWED SENSE OF OWNERSHIP

Many of us who came up through the ranks at ING shared a common experience: we had weathered the crisis together. And coming out the other side, we felt a renewed sense of ownership. We weren't just employees; we felt like stewards of the bank. We believed in what ING could be, and we saw the post-crisis period as a chance to rebuild something better.

Society was saying, "You're not the good guys." And internally, we were saying, "Yes, we are."

But how do you prove that?

There was a strong sense that we needed to do things differently. That we had to show, not just say, that ING could be better than before.

What I said to the team at the time was this: "We are fundamentally a beautiful company. But the world doesn't see that right now. That's okay. Let's show them. Not through slogans or declarations but through actions. Through the way we serve customers. Through the way we rebuild. Through how we show up, every day."

It wasn't about being loud. It was about being proud. And proving, with humility and consistency, who we really were.

We fully delivered on that, which based on our continuous customer growth and a rapidly increased number of primary clients, is something I can see more clearly now.

LISTENING TO CUSTOMERS

"You think you know what customers want. You don't. Go find out. Assumptions kill businesses. Start by listening, not guessing."

—BRUNON BARTKIEWICZ, FORMER CEO OF ING POLAND

Once we regained our footing, the starting point was clear: we would put the customer first, again. This time, we would do it at scale. For this, we couldn't rely on our history. We had to listen. Not to our assumptions but to our customers themselves. If we were going to restore trust and rebuild around a renewed sense of purpose, we needed to start with their stories.

- What did people really want from their bank?
- What had gone wrong?
- What role were they still hoping we could play in their lives?

What stood out in the research was that all the stories centered around trust. The negative stories were about banks in general, and the positive stories were about the bank playing a very relevant role in the lives and businesses of their customers.

That insight was powerful. It reminded us that rebuilding trust wasn't just about reputation repair; it was about reestablishing meaningful relationships. If trust had been lost because the industry had grown distant and disconnected, then earning it back meant becoming close again.

It didn't matter that ING Direct had always operated on customer-first principles. Perception doesn't always follow intent; the damage was done. We were seen as part of the problem.

So we had to start over. We had to rebuild trust from the ground up.

As we say in Dutch, *vertrouwen komt te voet en gaat te paard*: trust arrives on foot and leaves on horseback. It takes years to build and only a moment to lose.

That became our challenge and our mission. We had to prove, slowly and deliberately, that we were different. That we truly did put the customer at the center of everything we did. That it was about them, not about us. That proof, those actions, those experiences, became the foundation for everything we would build going forward.

> *"Other banks failed in the digital transformation, because they were organized around products and channels. When customers started interacting differently, the business model didn't change fast enough to truly understand them."*
>
> —IGNACIO JULIÁ VILAR, FORMER ING GLOBAL HEAD OF RETAIL

ROOTED IN THE REAL ECONOMY

I believe that banks have always cared about people. Banking, at its core, is about relationships, helping individuals buy homes, build businesses, and plan. Somewhere along the way, particularly in the lead-up to the 2008 financial crisis, that connection began to fray.

Part of the problem was the environment. Many bankers spent their entire careers surrounded only by others in the financial world. Their networks, conversations, and daily reality revolved around hedge funds, investors, and capital markets. Over time, that closed loop became their version of the "real world," and the true customer side of banking faded into the background. They were banking for banking's sake, seeking arbitrage of regulations and risk models.

At the time, many of the people who ended up in the leadership of banks came up through trading or investment banking. Their focus wasn't the real economy; it was making the financial system itself more efficient or profitable.

My experience was different.

I started my career as a corporate banker. From the very beginning, I was working directly with clients, trying to understand their businesses, their challenges, and how we could help them grow. That's what I did for the first fifteen years of my career. Every day was focused on one question: how can we help this customer?

That shaped how I see the role of a bank. I spent my time learning about real industries, oil and gas, power generation, aviation, shipping, even film financing. These were companies creating real value in the economy, and my job was to figure out how to support them. That was the world I grew up in.

Our Strategy on a Page didn't open with a financial ambition, shareholders' value, or a market dominance statement. It began with the customer.

It said, "This is our purpose. This is our customer promise. These are our priorities."

That was the strategy, entirely customer-focused, by design.

It was remarkably simple.

Creating a differentiating customer experience

▶ Strategic
Priorities

1 Earn the primary relationship
2 Develop analytics skills to understand our customers better
3 Increase the pace of innovation to serve changing customer needs
4 Think beyond traditional banking to develop new services and business models

Our strategy was about creating a differentiated customer experience. It was about building a bank around knowing the customer and delivering the right service, not products or structures or financial engineering.

If you look at the four strategic priorities we defined, each one ties directly to the customer:

1. Earn primary relationships by delivering a distinctive customer experience.
2. Use data and analytics to understand customers more deeply.
3. Accelerate innovation to meet changing customer needs.
4. Go beyond banking to create new services and stay relevant in customers' lives.

Customers were at the spine of the entire strategy. Even our purpose, "Empowering people to stay ahead in life and business," was centered around helping the customer succeed.

A Customer at the Core ideology for ING wasn't a pivot for me; it was a return to form. For ING, it was a reaffirmation of who we had always been at our best.

Translating that strategy into reality required more than just a shift in vision. It required a shift in how the organization operated. Putting the customer at the center couldn't remain an abstract goal. It had to show up in our structure, our culture, and our daily decisions.

CUSTOMER-CENTRIC VALUE

One of the most critical shifts we made was transforming the role of the head office from being distant into an active driver of a customer-centric strategy.

During the restructuring years, the head office had to stay removed from the day-to-day operations to make tough, often painful decisions: what to sell, what to keep, what to cut. That distance was necessary for survival, but it also created a gap between strategy development and customer reality. The center made strategy decisions, but the real work, the client engagement, the product delivery, the innovation, was happening in the operating companies beneath it.

In the beginning of the Think Forward strategy (2014–2016), we redefined the operating companies as the core storytellers of the business. They were the ones closest to the customer. That's where the customer promise needed to live. That's where the transformation had to start.

To support that shift, we restructured how priorities were set and how progress was measured. Local leaders had more autonomy to shape experiences that reflected their customer base. The center still provided strategic direction but also measured the local progress into the more aligned direction.

Transforming the structure and culture of the organization was only part of the shift. As we looked ahead, another challenge quickly emerged: how do we carry that customer closeness into a world where branches are disappearing and most interactions happen through a screen?

Beyond, how do we move from large screen (internet) banking, with a low frequency of interaction with our customers, to small screen (mobile) banking, with several interactions per day with our customers?

REINVENTING THE HUMAN TOUCH

How do we understand our customer if we no longer meet them face to face?

Even more importantly: how do we ensure that our service still feels personal in a digital world?

To answer that, we leaned into one of our core strategic priorities: leveraging digital data and analytics to understand customer needs more deeply and serve them more personally.

In the old world, a local branch manager knew their customers intuitively. They lived in the same village, saw each other on the street, and sat next to one another in church. The banker shopped at the local supermarket and could tell when something wasn't quite right. That physical presence created a natural feedback loop. Out of a duty of care, which has always been fundamental to our role as bankers, that branch manager could step in and help when needed.

In a digital world, those physical signals disappear. Customers become numbers in a system.

For me, the challenge was clear: how do we retain that same attentiveness and care without the in-person cues?

Let me give a concrete example.

Imagine a customer with a mortgage whose salary is deposited with us. Month after month, we see the inflow. Then, suddenly, the salary stops.

In the past, a banker might have heard on the street that

the local plant was closing or that someone had lost their job. But in a digital world, they don't hear it; they must see it. That missing salary becomes a data signal.

The banker waits another month to confirm it wasn't a one-off. When the inflow doesn't resume, that's a trigger.

A good banker doesn't wait for the customer to fall behind on mortgage payments. Instead, they reach out proactively to fulfill their duty of care: "We've noticed a change in your financial situation. Let's talk. You have a mortgage with us. Should we explore restructuring options together?"

That's what it means to recreate the human touch through data. We didn't innovate for the sake of it; we innovated to make banking better: more responsive, more personal, and more supportive.

This was our way of carrying our duty of care into the digital age. With the right insights, tools, and mindset, we could still understand our customers, not by seeing them on the street but by recognizing their needs in real time and reaching out when relevant.

At the same time, banks had to be cautious as to how to use data. Given the quickly changing world, new regulation was needed to ensure data was used with consent, confidentially, and ethically.

But done right, digital banking could feel just as personal as before, sometimes even more so. While redesigning the customer experience, we launched the PIRS principle for customer experience: the experience should be Personal, Instant, Relevant, and Seamless. In the next chapter, we will explain how the PIRS principle guided the development of customer journeys, processes, and products.

REDEFINING BANKING FOR THE MOBILE ERA

Customer centricity had always been part of ING's DNA, but by the time we emerged from the crisis, the world had changed. So had our customers.

The mobile phone rapidly became ubiquitous. In 2015, the Apple Watch was released. Mobile banking became increasingly popular. This wasn't just a new delivery channel; it marked a deeper shift: banking was no longer a static product. It had become a dynamic activity. Something people do, not just something they have.

That distinction changed everything; it became central to our strategy.

We weren't interested in simply digitalizing traditional banking. We wanted to redefine what banking meant in the lives of our customers. Our innovation efforts began to focus on how we could make everyday services—checking balances, making payments, tracking spending—not just accessible but seamless, intuitive, and proactive. It was about developing customer journeys as simple and intuitively as possible so customers could do everything themselves, through intuitive simple processes, transparent products, and instant delivery if possible.

When Nanne Bos, then head of brand, pushed to divert the traditional advertising budget into improving the user experience, I wasn't convinced at first.

"In the past, branding was about getting in the minds of people; today branding is about being relevant in the *lives or businesses* of people. So it makes sense to shift from traditional advertising to digital experience," he said.

I eventually supported it, but it went against typical marketing strategy and required courage.

The vision was clear: your banking app should work like your health app. It should alert you if your salary hasn't arrived, if you're nearing the end of your monthly budget, or if something unusual shows up in your spending. It should be part of your daily rhythm, something you check alongside the weather, the news, or the stock market. Similar features should be developed for payments and cash management of corporate customers, like a dashboard of real-time money flows.

We expected mobile banking to become the norm. That insight reshaped our priorities. We weren't just building better interfaces; we were embedding banking into the flow of daily life or business. Relevance, usability, and integration became our North Stars.

From that point forward, every innovation had to make banking effortless, contextual, and deeply personal.

ELEVATING THE DIGITAL EXPERIENCE THROUGH INNOVATION

Throughout my time at ING, and continuing to this day, we placed enormous emphasis on ensuring our digital experience was truly best-in-class. We had a clear insight early on: a superior digital experience shapes customer behavior. It builds loyalty, reduces friction, and creates trust.

That realization became a core driver of our innovation agenda. The first way to innovate, more organically, was through the introduction of the agile way of working; we innovated and improved on a continuous basis. Delivering incremental changes, new functionality, etc., very quickly. Test something new and move on quickly if it fails.

We didn't stop at improving our own services, however. We started looking beyond ING's existing brand and offerings. Our model was to deliver the client the right product, not necessarily our own. But if we were the bank through which clients would interact, they would see us as their gateway for their financial needs. This is referred to as "platform banking."

So we invited employees to think beyond traditional banking. We wanted innovation to come from within, not just top-down.

The second way to innovate was through inviting our colleagues to come up with completely new ideas. We launched internal bootcamps where, every few months, people could pitch ideas. These ideas would be reviewed, and a couple would be selected for further development. The team received funding and full responsibility to bring those ideas to life (proof of concept, or PoC) in our own Accelerator Labs across the globe (Amsterdam, Brussels, London, Singapore). At the end of each bootcamp cycle, a jury of internal and external leaders would select which PoC would receive investment to become a separate service or even company.

This wasn't innovation for innovation's sake. Like the introduction of agile, it was a deliberate move away from the old ways of banking and toward a future where creativity, agility, and customer relevance were the norm. And by empowering our people to drive that change, we made innovation part of the culture, not just a department.

To support innovation across the organization, and to help colleagues bring their ideas to life through bootcamps, we set up our own Accelerator Labs and developed ING's own structured innovation method, called PACE. It's a five-phase process that combines the best components of Design Thinking, Agile Scrum, and Lean Startup methodologies.

One notable success was Yolt, an open banking initiative in the UK, launched in 2017 that gave users a holistic view of their finances by connecting multiple financial service providers in a single app. We built a similar aggregation model for our wholesale banking clients a year earlier, in 2016, called Cobase. Today, Cobase is a successful independent multibank platform.

We also innovated in the payments space. In 2014, we launched Payconiq, a day-to-day payment app in the Netherlands and Belgium. It became Belgium's payment standard. In Spain, we introduced TWYP (The Way You Pay) in 2015, an app designed for small peer-to-peer payments.

Our ambition went beyond banking as well. Inspired by ING Netherlands "Rentepuntenwinkel," we launched ING Bazar in Romania in 2014, offering users discounts and shopping deals. That platform evolved into Dealwise, now active in Germany and other countries. In wholesale banking, one bootcamp idea became Komgo, the largest multibank trade finance platform developed on blockchain and the market leader in digital trade services, based in Switzerland. Other successes were Sparq and Pyctor.

Of course, not every initiative was a success. But that's the nature of innovation. Like in agile, we had to make failure part of our culture, if we learned from it. For example, Yolt was a commercial success, but it was difficult to make it a financial success.

We also recognized that we didn't have a monopoly on good ideas. So, alongside our internal bootcamps, labs, and agile way of working, we wanted to make sure we didn't miss promising innovations from outside the company.

As a third way to innovate for our clients, we launched a €300 million innovation fund, ING Ventures in 2017. Through this fund, we invested in startups and emerging technologies, either to support promising standalone businesses or to integrate exciting new capabilities into our customer journeys. The investments we made earlier were transferred to this fund.

This marked a cultural shift: embracing innovation from third parties, investing in early-stage companies, and remaining open to both success and failure in the venture space.

We were early investors in companies like:

- Twisto (2017), a buy-now-pay-later service that is now part of the larger personal finance platform Param
- Kabbage for SME lending (2015), later acquired by American Express
- WeLab (2016), a digital lending platform powered by machine learning

Not all investments were a success. As part of our ambition to build platform banking, we made a small acquisition with Payvision in the Netherlands. The idea was to accelerate ING's proposition in the payments business by buying it to get access to the latest technology. Although it looked promising at first, its legacy business caused some major issues. ING announced the wind down of the business in 2021.

These investments signaled not just a new approach to

product development but a mindset of continuous exploration, external collaboration, and experimentation.

ALIGNING THE WHOLESALE BANK WITH A CUSTOMER-FIRST STRATEGY

As the culture of innovation took hold, enthusiasm spread quickly across much of the organization. While the spirit of the transformation was widely embraced, not everyone saw themselves clearly reflected in the strategy, at first. For our retail banking teams, the direction felt intuitive, but for our wholesale banking colleagues, the translation wasn't as immediate. That's where the next layer of work began: making sure every part of the business, not just consumer-facing units, could see their role in the customer-first future we were building.

For wholesale bankers who have frequent face-to-face customer contact, the resistance wasn't philosophical; it was interpretive. The teams didn't feel fully reflected in the narrative or the framing of the strategic priorities. The role wholesale bankers play in adding value to their customers through content was of course crucial.

However, ensuring that the solutions they offered in lending, payments and cash management, trade finance, and markets were delivered in an easy, transparent, direct, and fast way, without operational hiccups, was just as important. It took more effort, more explanation, and more tailored conversations to help them see themselves in the story. It came with the realization that the improvement of the delivery, not just the content/advice, also was the responsibility of the bankers. Having the best advice with a poor and accident-prone delivery undermined their credibility. Once they realized that, alignment quickly followed and enthusiasm spread fast, evidenced by the successes in innovation.

What we were building was deeply connected to everything else, our purpose, our positioning, our brand, our growth agenda, our innovation agenda, our shift to agile, our culture, the need for different capabilities. It boosted the level of employee engagement across the organization, because the energy behind it was palpable. The invitation we extended—to think differently, to reimagine what banking could be—ignited the organization. It changed how people saw their jobs and gave them permission to contribute in new ways. The shift in energy, in belief, in ownership, it was massive.

It also changed how others outside the company viewed us. We were no longer a traditional bank; we were becoming recognized as a digital player, a company driving real transformation. We began attracting talent across all countries in which we were active, from far beyond the banking industry, people who were inspired by the story we were telling and wanted to be part of it.

That was rare. It reminded me of companies like Nike or other deeply customer-centric brands. There was a certain magic in what we were doing, something magnetic about the mission, the momentum, and the culture.

When we first began speaking about banking and innovation in the same breath, it challenged expectations. Those words didn't belong together, until we made them belong. Through the energy we created, belief followed, and that belief is what transformed the culture, from the inside out.

BRINGING MONEY20/20 TO AMSTERDAM

As confirmation of our belief in a digital future, in 2016, I attended Money20/20 in Copenhagen, the European arm of the largest banking innovation conference in the world. Being on stage as the only incumbent at the time and seeing the fintechs presenting, it convinced me of one thing: *we had to bring this conference to Amsterdam where our head office is.* We were asked by representatives from the Amsterdam municipality, who were already discussing this, to help convince Money20/20 to move from Copenhagen to Amsterdam. This move, in addition to ING's frequent appearances on the Money20/20 stages in Las Vegas and Singapore, also improved our reputation so we were able to attract top digital and engineering talent.

ALL THANKS TO CUSTOMER LOYALTY

I'm sure I said it in many speeches at the time, because I truly believed it: if it hadn't been for the loyalty of our customers, ING would not have survived.

In the darkest moments of the crisis, when trust in the banking sector had collapsed, our customers stayed. They didn't walk away. They didn't withdraw their deposits or take their business elsewhere. That loyalty wasn't something we could take for granted. It was a lifeline.

Yes, there was a widespread loss of trust in banks, but much of that was driven by systemic issues, capital structures, and regulatory uncertainty, not necessarily by the actions of individual institutions. In our case, even as we were swept up in the larger narrative, our customers continued to believe in us as ING and our employees who made the difference.

That loyalty gave us the time and space we needed to recover, and it gave us a responsibility.

If our customers had remained loyal through the most difficult period in our history, who were we not to return that loyalty?

We owed them everything, and we never forgot that.

THE CUSTOMER IN THE BOARDROOM

Before I took over, the customer and what we needed to do for them, especially on the retail side, occasionally came up in the boardroom, not from a strategic or commercial perspective but from a regulatory one. That was certainly important, but not sufficient.

We had to add more dimensions.

Every topic that came to the board was required to include a cover sheet outlining the impact on customers. We made it standard practice to ask:

- How does this decision contribute to our purpose?
- What does it mean for the people and companies we serve?
- How do we make this work?
- Are we staying true to who we say we are?

It wasn't just a procedural checkbox; it was a cultural shift.

Although it was important in board meetings to continue discussing risk matters like capital and liquidity ratios, trading limits, credit exposures, compliance, and operational stability, we added other subjects to have comprehensive discussions on customer need and impact of our decisions. We brought the discussion back to include the customer at the center of board-level decision-making, one of the clearest signals that ING was changing.

In the end, everything we built, our purpose, our strategy, our digital innovations, even our internal culture, came back to one simple truth: it's not about us. It's about the people we serve. That belief shaped how we led, how we listened, and how we rebuilt trust from the ground up.

We didn't need to be the loudest. We needed to be the most dependable. Quietly indispensable. Like trust itself.

The better we did our job, the less we were noticed, and the more progress our customers could make in their business or own lives. That, to me, is what banking should be. So that's what we returned to, and it's what continued to guide us forward.

We were earning trust back by putting the customer at the center. Now we had to build the infrastructure that would make that promise real.

THE BLUEPRINT OF A DIGITAL BANK

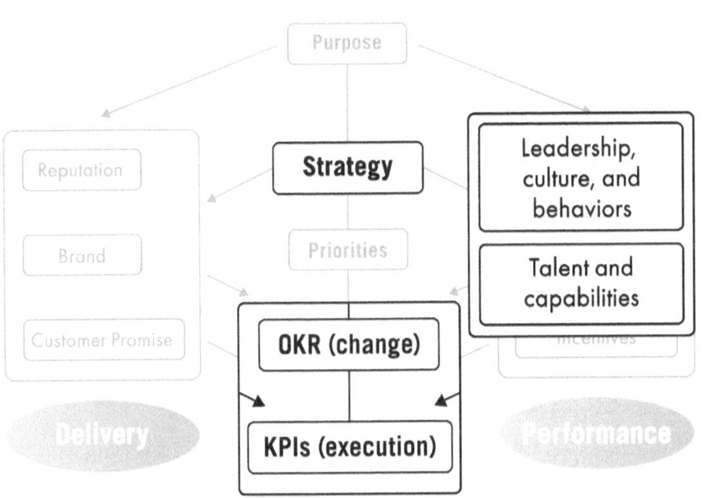

I brought Roel Louwhoff into ING in 2014 as our chief operations officer (COO). He was one of my first external hires. He'd led transformation work outside banking, in telecom to be more precise, an industry that was purely about technology and driven by constant change. Roel was needed to generate a different perspective. He took one look at how we operated and said what I needed to hear.

"Ralph, you have the technology," he told me. "You have the people. You have the money. But this is not a technology project."

I leaned back. "Then what is it?"

"Organizational fragmentation. The problem isn't building digital capability. The problem is getting people to build it together, on shared platforms, with shared standards."

He meant it literally. ING wasn't one bank. It was a collection of isolated worlds (countries, functions, systems) each protecting its own way of working.

I knew exactly what he meant.

"So what's the blueprint?" I asked.

Roel didn't hesitate. "We stop rewarding reinvention. We build horizontal platforms that everyone uses."

"And if they resist?" I asked.

He gave me a look. "They will."

He was right.

Not long after, a senior country leader told us directly: "I don't support this. I want to run my own operating model."

I asked him, "Are you saying you want your own bank inside our bank?"

He didn't blink. "Yes."

That was the moment the blueprint stopped being conceptual. If we let that stand, we would never build one digital ING. We would keep funding duplication forever (different apps, different stacks, different road maps) while digital competitors scaled one experience.

We agreed to disagree…and we agreed he should leave.

After that, everything in our digitalization agenda became clearer.

Because becoming a digital bank was about breaking the logic of silos, building shared platforms, and aligning leaders around a single standard: if it can't be reused, it can't be scaled.

That's where the blueprint began.

THINKING DIFFERENTLY

Becoming a truly digital bank isn't just about adopting new technologies. It's about thinking differently, about who you are, what you offer, and how you deliver it. At ING, we realized early on that transformation required a radical shift in both mindset and infrastructure. We needed to simplify the experience, standardize the way we operated across countries, and rewire the technology behind it all. But none of that would matter if we didn't bring our people along for the ride. Engineers needed to be empowered to build. Leaders needed to believe in the new model. And the organization needed a shared environment, physically and philosophically, that allowed everyone to align, move faster, and innovate together. This chapter outlines how we designed that blueprint: what we built, how we worked, and why it changed ING at its core.

THE CUSTOMER OF THE FUTURE

We knew that people no longer visited banks and saw our logo over a branch.

If clients no longer visit branches, how do you ensure they know about your bank, let alone find you? The answer is simple: you have to be where they are.

Today, customers spend their time online scrolling through Facebook and Instagram, ordering meals through apps, shopping for clothes on Zalando or Amazon. Small business clients order supplies, electricity, and services digitally. If we want to remain relevant, we need to be embedded in that digital supply chain. That means integrating with these platforms or, in some cases, even owning them.

Take housing, for example. Clients searching online for homes will eventually need a mortgage. But how can we detect that they're in the market before they even realize they'll need us? That's the opportunity: to meet them at the moment of need, not after the fact.

As discussed in the previous chapter, we shifted from a product-centric to a client-centric model...from a focus on savings to a focus on the primary relationship. We moved from infrequent, large-screen banking to frequent, mobile-first interactions. The smartphone made it possible to become a complete bank digitally, without the need for branches.

Even more: the more frequently clients interacted with us, the better we got to know them. The better we knew them, the more proactive we could be. The more relevant we became, the more they liked us, and the cycle continued. We found a strong correlation between payment account usage, frequency of interaction, and the likelihood of clients buying additional products.[6]

In this world, I began to speak not of cross-selling but of cross-buying. The client is in control, actively buying products, not being sold to. They're already on a journey, shopping, moving, investing, and we must be ready to serve them in that moment. Be there. Be relevant. Be personal. Deliver instantly and seamlessly. PIRS.

The questions became:

1. How do we guide our current customers to new digital ways of being supported by ING?
2. How do we reach the digital customer of the future and show up where they already are?
3. Once we're there, how do we become meaningful in the exact moment they need us?
4. If they use us, how do we become invisible yet indispensable?

Those were the four steps.

BE WHERE THE CLIENT IS

We needed to become part of the ecosystems people were already using to meet their basic needs, like buying a home. That's why, in the Netherlands in 2018, we acquired a digital housing broker, Makelaarsland, something like Zillow with a broker function. We made that move because we knew that's where the customer journey was starting. If someone is looking for a house, that's where they'll go. If we can see them revisiting the same listing multiple times, we can reasonably infer they're considering a purchase. If they're considering a purchase, they'll need a mortgage. That's the moment we need to be present, before they even think to search for a bank.

Here's the thing, though: that didn't work. After engaging with the platform, many customers stepped out of the process and checked with mortgage brokers. "Before I decide on ING for my mortgage, I'm going to check with a few other banks." This character of the Dutch market we were unable to change. ING decided to sell its stake to the management of Makelaarsland in 2021.

Another example: let's say a consumer is shopping online and reaches the checkout page. How do we insert ING into that moment? It's about being where the customer is, at the right time, in the right context.

We couldn't rely on brand visibility anymore; we had to be embedded in the journey itself.

THE PRINCIPLE OF SIMPLICITY

As our technology matured and we became faster at building and deploying solutions, a new challenge emerged: just because we could build something didn't mean we should. Speed and scale were powerful, but they had to be guided by something deeper: a clear understanding of what mattered to the customer.

One of the core principles that guided our digital transformation was understanding the difference between engineering the perfect solution and engineering the perfect *experience*. It was about *how*, not about *what*.

As shared earlier, if we wanted to empower people, whether in their personal lives or their businesses, we had to create experiences that were invisible yet indispensable. Can a bank be so functional that the customer hardly notices its service yet, without it, can't complete a primary need, like purchasing a product?

That idea became something of a mantra for me. It captured the heart of customer-centric design, and we knew it needed to be embedded in everything we built.

The challenge, of course, was rooted in human nature. Engineers—brilliant, creative, driven—tend to chase perfection. So do bankers. Perfect solutions, however, are often overly complex, and complexity is the enemy of usability. Our goal wasn't perfection. It was functionality. What works. 80 percent.

THE PIRS PRINCIPLE

The world was moving ever faster, in my view, too fast for a 100 percent perfect solution. By the time you reach it, the world has already shifted. In truth, we never actually get to 100 percent. Outside of risk and compliance solutions, 80 percent is as close as we can reasonably aim for, and we have to be okay with that. We could improve from there after the service was live.

This mindset was especially critical in retail banking. We called this the PIRS principle, which needed to apply to the development of customer journeys, processes, and products:

- Personal
- Instant
- Relevant
- Seamless

That's why simplicity wasn't just a design principle. It became a leadership challenge. To build experiences that felt effortless to the customer, we had to introduce a level of discipline and alignment internally.

Simplicity couldn't only live in theory; it had to show up in the products we offered. If our goal was to create intuitive, transparent experiences, we needed to strip away the noise at the core of our business. That meant rethinking what we offered and why. We couldn't expect to deliver seamless digital journeys if the underlying product catalog was bloated, confusing, or filled with legacy offerings that no longer made sense. So we asked a fundamental question: what do customers need?

FIVE CORE PRODUCTS

ING Direct was always run with disciplined simplicity in both processes and products. Any new product idea had to demonstrate strong potential before it was even considered.

- Did clients truly need it?
- Would it genuinely add to our offering?
- Would it make us more complex?

When I took over, ING had many branch banking operations in countries like the Netherlands, Belgium, Luxembourg, Poland, Romania, and Turkey. Over the years, these banks had developed a broad and extensive product shelf. Once products were introduced, they continued to be offered and had to be maintained technically and updated to comply with new laws and regulations.

But what if we cut down that enormous shelf and simplified it?

That question sparked a major simplification initiative in our journey: we narrowed our offering down to five core product categories, reducing complexity, lowering costs, and minimizing compliance risks.

If you think about it from a customer's perspective, most people only need five financial products: a payment account, a savings account, a personal loan or credit card, an investment account or brokerage account (especially in the US), and a mortgage. That's it.

Not 100+ variations on these products like many banks offered at the time. Why would you have ten different salary accounts? It didn't make sense. Also, we needed to clean it up with digital delivery in mind.

If there is no advisor, and clients need to choose (and need to understand the products themselves), the *products* need to be transparent and do what they promise to do.

Most people don't have the time, capacity, or interest to wade through that complexity. They don't understand it. They shouldn't have to. The experience should be transparent and honest, without hidden conditions or fine print designed to trip them up.

By narrowing our focus, we laid the foundation for a simpler, more customer-centric offering. Simplification wasn't just about cutting down the catalog, though. It was about how those products were delivered and experienced.

SIMPLE BANKING IS NOT SIMPLE TO DO.

For larger wholesale banking clients, this became our standard for delivering services in the transactional environment. In areas like structured finance, financial markets, and investment banking, tailored advice and bespoke products remained essential, but just as critical was flawless execution. Even the best advice could lose credibility if the operational delivery had hiccups, as indicated in the previous chapter.

SMEs were also embracing digital tools for their day-to-day banking needs. But they increasingly expected more than just basic banking; they were looking for complementary services like accounting and other operational tools delivered in a seamless digital experience.

That gave us a chance to think beyond traditional banking. What if, for example, we could support their procurement, not just their finances?

We knew that SMEs, when handling their day-to-day procurement—whether it was printer paper, purchasing coffee for the office, or accounting services—were already going online. So we built digital ecosystems specifically for those needs. We launched such a platform successfully in Poland (ING Aleo, 2015) and Romania.

By creating an online hub where they could easily compare prices, manage orders, and access essential services, we made their lives easier. In doing so, we kept ING front and center. We weren't just a bank; we were part of their operating rhythm.

Today, that feels standard, but back then, it was ahead of the curve.

Because the platform carried our brand, it created more openness to working with us financially. We met SMEs where they were, supporting their real, immediate needs, and sometimes, that got them back in service with us as a bank.

CONVERGENCE ACROSS COUNTRIES

The Think Forward strategy had established a clear purpose, well-defined strategic priorities, a globally consistent brand positioning (over time, see Chapter 9: Living the Brand), and a unified customer promise. Within the wholesale bank, which was managed functionally across more than forty countries, this translated into a technology initiative called the Wholesale Banking Target Operating Model. Standardizing the technology enabled standardization in the delivery of products and services across markets.

In the retail bank, however, we initially left the translation of the standardized purpose, brand positioning, and customer promise to each country. Our goal was to build commercial momentum by shifting from product-focused to primary client relationships, and this localized approach delivered good results. This was the first phase of Think Forward (2014–2016), which we also used to simplify our products and processes. The local execution strategy, however, led to variants of our brand, customer promise, and experience. They were not the same.

To achieve consistency and relevance at scale, however, we couldn't continue building market by market. We needed to align the entire organization behind a single vision: one experience, one model.

If we truly wanted to become a digital bank, one brand, one user experience, one promise to the customer, we had to converge our operations across all countries into a single model as well.

That was one part of the equation.

A TECHNOLOGY COMPANY WITH A BANKING LICENSE

The other was redefining how we saw ourselves. We had to stop thinking like a bank with IT systems and start thinking like a tech company with a banking license. Technology couldn't only be an enabler; it had to become a *differentiator*.

In a digital bank, the customer experience is entirely shaped by how they interact with you. That interaction happens through technology. There's no branch manager watching your expression or tone of voice. There's no one reading your body language. It all comes down to how the technology performs and how well it's designed to meet the customer's needs.

If you want to unify across countries, you must commit to one model and one *experience.*

Then, you must clean up your core systems to support that ambition. It wasn't just about converging systems anymore; it was about designing an experience that could meet real-world expectations in real time.

Standardization became the quiet force behind everything we were building. It was about enabling consistency at scale. By aligning our tools, platforms, and technology architecture across countries, we could create a shared foundation that allowed us to move faster, reuse more, and deliver a unified customer experience regardless of geography. At the same time, standardization could help with risk management and compliance challenges tremendously as well. Standardization didn't mean sameness; it meant interoperability. It gave our teams the ability to innovate locally while building from a common base. And for our customers, it meant that no matter where they interacted with ING, the experience felt intuitive, reliable, and distinctly ours.

A technology reboot was necessary, and that kind of shift is never easy. It requires significant investment in an area where the return isn't always clear.

After three years of Think Forward (2014–2016), we decided to accelerate the implementation of our strategy and launched *Accelerate* Think Forward early October 2016.

As part of this launch, I gave a speech outlining our vision for becoming One Digital Bank: a scalable, customer-centric platform with global standards and simplified operations. This wasn't a hypothetical end-state. It was a call to action.

The idea was to standardize the user experience across countries, delivering on our customer promise and one brand. Also, technology, risk management, and data management needed to be the same to reuse models. Only the product layer needed local tweaks because of habits, tax treatment or specific regulations, not unlike the approach by Facebook, Instagram, or Amazon. The experience is the same everywhere, but the fulfillment of your actual need (product, short video, etc.) is local.

That moment forced me to be very direct, first with myself and then with the organization. If we were serious about saving customers time and simplifying their lives, we had to start by simplifying ourselves. We could not continue to ask people to navigate complexity on the outside while we protected it on the inside.

We had become increasingly convinced that a consistent customer experience across borders was impossible without real cross-border collaboration inside the bank. For too long, we had accepted that doing things differently in every country was a sign of local strength. It was also a source of inefficiency and fragmentation. In several markets, we simply did not have the Sustainable Share to digitalize independently. If we wanted to compete in a digital world, we had to share solutions, technology, and ways of working.

That meant accepting a difficult truth: our apps and platforms could no longer be built around local silos. They had to serve universal customer needs. It meant changing my own mindset from country-first to platform-first. That shift was not theoretical. It required simplifying, streamlining, and standard-izing across products, systems, and services.

One platform. One foundation. One shared approach to data, processes, and architecture.

We began taking concrete steps in that direction. Cross-border collaboration between the Netherlands and Belgium across many areas, and later between Spain, France, and Italy, became intermediate milestones, proof points that sharing solutions was not only possible but beneficial. Other markets, including Germany and Australia, continued developing plans that would allow them to benefit from common technology over time, unless there was an obvious opportunity to accelerate, like the One App development between the Netherlands, Belgium, and Germany.

Wholesale banking showed us what platform-scale service could look like when alignment, technology, and execution came together. A shared platform also allowed us to open up through global APIs, enabling co-creation with fintechs and wholesale partners in ways that were simply not possible before.

None of this was abstract. We invested €800 million to reach this intermediate state because the benefits were tangible: €2.3 billion in additional revenue, €900 million in cost reductions, and faster, cheaper, more empowering service for customers. Transformation also had a human cost. More than 7,000 roles were impacted along the way. From the start, we committed to handling every transition with care, support, and respect. That mattered, not just ethically but culturally.

That moment marked another turning point. It clarified that digital transformation is not primarily about technology. It is about alignment, having the courage to make hard choices, and staying anchored in purpose while changing how an entire organization operates.

THE PARADOX OF STANDARDIZATION

Everyone loved the idea of standardization, at least in theory. The vision was clear: offer the same experience to our customers everywhere. Same logo. Same services. Even the same cards.

Everyone agreed that we could, and should, standardize the customer experience, just like Apple, Google, and Meta had shown to be successful.

People liked that idea and believed in the concept. They appreciated the story we were building. Everyone loved the shiny toy.

Then came the reality.

To deliver that kind of consistency, we needed standardization in almost everything. What the customer sees and how the organization operates, which meant aligning everything: the underlying technology, how we worked with technology, how finance, HR, and operations worked. That's when resistance showed up. They wanted the unified customer experience, but when it came to doing standardized work, the questions began.

"Wait, you're going to prescribe *how* I do this? That's what you mean?"

"Yes. That's standardization."

It's a fascinating paradox. Some people, especially those from countries with a post-communist history, joked that it felt like a return to central planning. The irony is that standardization is *essential* for success in a capitalist environment.

- You can't scale without it.
- You can't identify what's working and what's not.
- You can't improve what you can't measure and compare.

The only way to unlock exponential growth at low marginal cost is by building on a common foundation.

The members of the Leadership Council said they were on board, but when the consequences became real, discomfort set in.

We tackled this by continuing to clarify the overall strategic direction and showing the example in other industries. The discomfort was understandable as country CEOs became country managers and needed to implement the strategy within the guardrails set and with centrally allocated technology investment budgets. This was not an easy message.

As they were all part of the Leadership Council, they knew the consequences of their own decision; some agreed with the direction but did not feel like the right leader for this next phase and decided to leave ING. Not immediately, but as the changes began taking shape.

WHOLESALE BANKING, A STANDARDIZATION LIGHTHOUSE

The funny thing was wholesale banking had already standardized across over forty countries. It was the model for retail to follow, which was still operating as a patchwork. In the retail world, every country had its own branding, its own systems, its own way of working. What "the bank" meant to customers varied depending on where you were. Twenty years ago, that was normal. When digital came in, that fragmentation started to feel outdated.

Naturally, I had colleagues who pushed back.

"But we're different," one said. "Banking is local."

"That's interesting," I said, "because the wholesale bank serves global clients, and we've already made it work there. Are you telling me an individual consumer needs more customization than a multinational corporation?"

Probably not.

I reminded them: "We're already doing this. Look at wholesale. It's the lighthouse." I even said it in a speech once.

"Don't tell me it's impossible. Just look at the wholesale bank."

Now we had to bring that same discipline to retail.

REAL-TIME STANDARDIZATION

The world was showing us standardization in retail could be done. Apple, Google, Facebook, Instagram, Spotify, Amazon: these were companies serving global users with a consistent experience. If we wanted to get there, we didn't have to invent something new. We just had to follow the path we'd already proven we could walk.

These are some of the steps we took.

STEP 1: INFRASTRUCTURE ALIGNMENT

The first step was infrastructure alignment.

When we talk about infrastructure, we're talking about foundational decisions about core systems, like moving from mainframe to cloud and standardizing the platforms we run the software on.

The infrastructure layer starts with processing: what kind of computing power we need, whether that's CPUs, mainframes, or cloud-based solutions.

All of this had to be done. It wasn't glamorous, but it was essential.

Clarity and simplicity on the front end, for both wholesale and retail digital banking, required bold decisions on the back end. If we wanted to deliver intuitive, seamless digital experiences, we needed a technology foundation that could support it. That's why we moved quickly to define the architecture beneath it all: a strategic roadmap that would modernize our core systems and create the conditions for a truly digital ING.

Ron van Kemenade, our chief information officer, had already worked with others to evaluate the path ahead:

- If this is what we want to build, what do we need to do to get there?
- Do we begin with the core systems?
- Do we move from mainframes to the emerging world of private or public cloud?

At the time, public cloud remained a point of debate, especially from a security standpoint. There were still open questions about whether banks would even be allowed to operate in the public cloud. So we chose to first move to the private cloud, which meant core systems like mainframes would be phased out.

Ron played a central role in architecting that shift. He guided the move first from mainframe to private cloud, and later to public cloud. But those changes addressed only the core infrastructure.

They didn't yet touch the customer experience, but they were a necessary condition.

Infrastructure is the first layer. The next is software.

STEP 2: STANDARDIZATION OF SOFTWARE

Which applications do we run on top of that infrastructure? More importantly, can we standardize them across all markets?

For example, in the wholesale bank—which, by nature, is international and demands consistency—we had different trading rooms running on different systems. That didn't make sense. A typical American bank ran a single system across the board. We needed to do the same. That shift became part of the earlier mentioned Wholesale Banking Target Operating Model: every country would migrate to the same system.

STEP 3: UNTANGLING THE SPAGHETTI

To truly operate as a digital bank, we had to address the messy, tangled reality sitting on top of that infrastructure: the complex, inconsistent ways our systems were connected. That was the next frontier. It wasn't just about what the technology ran on, nor the standardization of the software packages. It was about how it worked together, between software packages, between functions, between countries in the bank, etc. That meant confronting decades of patchwork connections, manual integrations, and siloed processes head-on.

We had to untangle the spaghetti.

That's where two new technology approaches (at that time) proved essential. We embraced them quickly.

APIs

The first was the emergence of APIs, application programming interfaces. These allowed one system to communicate with another through standardized connectors rather than building unique connections each time. At the time, this was a breakthrough.

Before APIs, most banks, like many large companies, were stuck with a tangled mess of connections. The call center system would connect to one data environment, which connected to a specific core banking system or piece of other software. The branch system had a different setup entirely, with its own data environment. Nothing was consistent. Everything was wired together manually, piece by piece, resulting in what we often described as a spaghetti bowl of connections.

We needed to untangle that, and APIs made it possible. They allowed us to isolate the systems, standardize the datasets, clean up the interfaces, and reconnect everything in a way that was faster, simpler, and far more scalable.

MICROSERVICES

Next, we began shifting our thinking in technology, moving away from big, monolithic processes toward something much more modular to a unified framework based on microservices: smaller, independent services that could run and evolve separately while still working together. Every single step in a process became its own microservice. This allowed us to develop, deploy, and update much faster. It was a foundational shift in how we built and ran the bank.

In greater detail, a microservice is a small, self-contained piece of code that performs a specific function, like onboarding a new customer, making a payment, or transferring money from a current account to a savings account. Each of these actions involves a sequence of technical steps, such as payment authorization or face recognition, that can be built independently.

Once a microservice was developed, it went on what we called "the shelf," a central repository where teams across countries could store and access reusable components. If Germany needed a payment microservice, for example, the team wouldn't rebuild it from scratch. They'd go to the shelf, find what had already been built by another market, and reuse it.

That simple rule, reuse before rebuilding, did several things: it saved money, drove standardization, improved the user experience, and enabled better operational risk management. In my 2016 speech, I said, "If this is where we want to go, we need to standardize, we need to collaborate, and we need to converge."

> *"We designed services people could reuse so they could spend time innovating, not rebuilding. Reusability was freedom. It unblocked creativity by eliminating redundancy."*
>
> —RON VAN KEMENADE, FORMER ING CHIEF INFORMATION OFFICER

BUILDING BELIEVERS AT THE COUNTRY LEVEL

As mentioned earlier, the first three years of my tenure as CEO were all about "Here's the strategy: go and execute it." The strategy gave the right direction; the execution was local. It got us moving.

The idea of standardization, becoming one, wasn't something I wrote behind a desk. It was a story we built together. The top team. The country managers. The Leadership Council. We crafted a shared narrative that made space for both contribution and consumption. That was essential. They weren't just expected to contribute what made their country unique; they were also expected to consume what others had developed. That was the point. We were all building a shared future.

Over time, proud, independent country managers were intentionally moved into new roles: positions where they could experience firsthand the power of a more centralized and standardized approach. Take Brunon, former CEO of ING Poland, for example. Before returning to manage Poland, he had worked at ING Direct and served as ING's chief innovation officer. He became a key leader in helping us drive innovation forward as part of Think Forward. That made a big difference.

His experience in those central roles transformed how he led when he returned to the country level. He could go back and say, "Yes, we're our own bank with our own regulator. But I helped build this. I believe in it. We need to contribute to the shelf, and we need to use what's on it."

He told the story in Poland. Another leader we'd moved through different leadership roles before returning told the same story in Spain. More followed. But it was far from easy to convince everyone of this direction.

That's how it works. That's why culture matters so much. Writing the strategy? That's easy. Getting buy-in? That's the hard part.

ZOOM OUT, ZOOM IN

Executing the strategy, standardizing across countries, and centrally prioritizing the full technology budget so we could avoid duplication required a completely different way of managing. In line with agile, we needed to build a synchronized rhythm for allocating technology capacity.

From my visits to Silicon Valley, I became convinced that we needed clarity on where we wanted to be in seven to nine years ("zoom out") while also planning the next three months of execution with the current and evolving context in mind ("zoom in"). The path to building a standardized bank was not a straight line. Economic conditions shifted. Laws and regulations evolved. Customer expectations continued to change.

In 2017, we introduced the practice of QBRs. These allowed

us to zoom out, reminding ourselves of our long-term direction while zooming in to reassess context and set clear priorities for the next quarter. Risk management and compliance always came first, "run the bank" second, "change the bank" third:

1. Risk, regulation, and compliance: This is your license to operate. If you do not manage risk properly and comply with regulations or the law, you simply cannot operate. Nothing else matters if this foundation fails.
2. Stability, maintenance, and availability ("run the bank"): Once licensed to operate, you must be predictable and reliable. Systems must work. Payments must clear. Clients must trust that the bank functions consistently every day.
3. Change, innovations, and growth ("change the bank"): Only after safety and stability are secured can you responsibly invest in transformation. Innovation is essential, but it must be driven by discipline and built on a solid base.

We communicated these priorities to the organization to guide the next three-month planning. For example, when we became aware of shortcomings in our processes around dealing with KYC, we prioritized and allocated much more capacity to this.

One month later, we conducted the QBR itself: we reviewed the previous quarter's projects, on time, on spec, on budget, and decided which projects would continue and which new ones could begin in the next three months.

THE OBEYA ROOM: MAKING THE INVISIBLE VISIBLE

To make this work, each executive team member needed to take responsibility and feel accountable for the progress within their division or function. They were required to present their own plans and updates, ensuring they personally led the execution of standardization across markets. There was nowhere to hide. If we truly wanted this transformation, we couldn't delegate the overall planning or execution to others. Ownership had to sit at the highest level.

Given the volume of projects and the global scale of ING's operations, we needed a shared space, one where all the moving parts could come together to manage our €1 billion discretionary technology investment budget.

That's where the Obeya room came in.

Obeya, which literally means "big room" in Japanese, was just that: a large physical space, where everything was on display.

- Our purpose, strategy, strategic priorities, customer promise
- Our high-level plans, timelines, OKRs, and KPIs
- The projects in flight
- The ones that were delayed
- The interdependencies between the projects that we needed to sort
- The costs/investment and return
- The decisions that we still needed to make
- A quarterly pulse check as to how the teams were doing

It was all there, visible and trackable, wall to wall.

We needed everyone in that room, especially my top team, because they were the ones communicating with their functions and divisions. They had to be able to say, "Your project is being paused for three months. We've decided, together, to redirect that capacity elsewhere. It's not just your capacity anymore. It's ours. We're building one thing."

That was the power of the Obeya room. You didn't have to

chase down updates or guess who was blocking progress. You just walked in and looked around. It made everything visible. And it made accountability real.

The actual location of the Obeya room was in the former vault of ING's head office. With all valuable documents like bonds, stocks, etc. dematerialized, it was empty. We decided to write another part of banking history, moving to digital, in that room.

CHIEF TRANSFORMATION OFFICER

Once we started implementing standardized technology projects from 2017 on, the next step was leveraging capacity across borders. If everyone was working the same way (see the next chapter), we could (theoretically) take a team from one country and have them support a project in another. Not just to reuse what had already been built but to accelerate progress where it mattered most.

Standardization made this possible. Everyone was using the same architecture, the same coding languages. Because we tracked each team's output, we knew their capabilities: their speed, their efficiency, their productivity. That gave us the ability to allocate resources across business divisions and countries, not just within them.

Of course, this meant sometimes giving and sometimes taking. We had agreed to build this together, and sometimes that meant focusing on one aspect of the build over another. From where the executive team sat, we could see the whole structure.

To manage this complexity, we set up a central transformation office, which required a new leadership role: the chief transformation officer, filled by Roel Louwhoff, who, next to his role as COO, was made responsible for orchestrating these efforts across the entire footprint.

Independent from the business divisions and functions, the central transformation office needed to be able to present the dilemmas around allocation. They also acted as a challenger, asking whether projects were truly making progress on their OKRs and whether those OKRs were leading to the intended KPIs.

Given the all-encompassing nature of this planning process, it was equally important to gather bottom-up feedback. We introduced quarterly pulse checks, allowing colleagues to share their state of mind, energy levels, and confidence in the transformation. This was crucial. They were empowered to execute and deliver, but they also needed to believe in the direction and feel supported in the journey.

A NEW ENGINEERING CULTURE

We also developed a culture aimed at attracting and maintaining the right engineering talent.

There's an old parable about three bricklayers. When asked what they're doing, the first says, "I'm laying bricks." The second says, "I'm building a wall." But the third looks up and says, "I'm building a cathedral." All three are doing the same task, but only one sees the bigger picture.

It's the same with engineers. If they believe they're only writing code or solving isolated problems, that's all the work will ever be. But if they understand the broader vision, what we're building, why it matters, and how it will shape customers' businesses or lives, they show up differently. They engage at a deeper level. They build with meaning, not just precision.

That was the power of ING's narrative at the time. We

weren't just writing code. We were building a digital bank unlike anything else. That message resonated. It helped us attract engineers who wanted to be part of something greater than what they could achieve on their own or working at another bank or even technology company.

It was essential to show them the bigger picture. We needed talent with the technical skill to execute the details but also the mindset to understand how those details fit into a larger vision. That combination is rare. Most engineers are trained to focus on the minutiae. Finding those who could zoom out, and feel energized by the broader ambition, was one of our biggest challenges.

We began sourcing global talent to raise the bar. When we brought them in, we put them on a pedestal. We invested in their development. We created a culture that recognized ingenuity, craftsmanship, and progression. We followed the Dreyfus model of skill acquisition. We have seen it work well. We made it clear that you could build a career here, not just a series of projects. Engineers were just as central to the bank's success as our bankers. The time when IT was viewed merely as a cost center was long behind us. Technology had become the key differentiator, and to succeed, we needed the best talent in the industry.

The goal was to make engineers proud to be engineers again. Not just task-completers. Not just freelancers hopping to the next highest bidder but professionals contributing to something bigger than themselves.

BRINGING EVERYONE ALONG

These ideas had to become part of the current engineers' mindsets, too. It wasn't just the marketers who needed to think this way: everyone had to internalize the customer-centric approach. The engineers, the product teams, the designers, they all needed to be connected to the purpose, brand, and customer promise. That is where agile came in.

From day one, I was responsible for taking 54,000 people along on this journey, many of whom had been with the bank for twenty or thirty years. This wasn't a clean-sheet startup. We didn't hire a brand-new team built perfectly for the future. With the people already in place, we needed to build something great.

We wanted all our colleagues to feel part of the story, not just implementers of someone else's vision.

That meant building an environment where one could see how their work contributed to a larger plan while still giving them space to explore and take initiative. We needed to be an attractive employer, not just by offering interesting problems but by showing them that their contributions mattered.

It all came back to empowerment: freedom to act with full accountability. That was the thread running through everything we were doing at the time. It was embedded in our purpose, reflected in the Orange Code, and needed to be genuinely felt by our people. The goal wasn't just to appeal to their creativity; it was to invite them into something bigger. We wanted people who were motivated by the opportunity to help build the new ING, a large fintech with a banking license.

That's what made this transformation so difficult and so meaningful at the same time. It wasn't only a technological shift. It was a cultural one. A reorientation around delivering for customers, by everyone, and thus, a new way of working.

THE ULTIMATE: FINANCES ON THE GO

Our blueprint was simplify the catalog, standardize the foundation, move to the cloud, standardize software, untangle the spaghetti, share as much code as possible, and empower people, from risk managers to engineers, from relationship managers to country managers. Every single colleague at ING needed to see the bigger picture and build it together.

It wasn't about making money. It was about building a true digital-primary client relationship.

It was about speed, shared direction, modernization, meaning, and purpose.

It was about building a bank that needed to work in real time and mattered in real life and in business. At every moment in the day.

That's what the blueprint made possible and what we kept refining, one experience, one model, one moment at a time.

> *"Banks traditionally have been built for a nine-to-five service... Changing all of your back-office systems from maybe daytime availability and nighttime processing into 24/7, always on and in real time, that is arguably the biggest effort."*
>
> —RON VAN KEMENADE, FORMER ING CHIEF INFORMATION OFFICER

BEST BANK IN THE WORLD

On October 16, 2017, ING was named *Best Bank in the World* by *Global Finance*. After four years of hard work by all our colleagues, we had delivered continuous momentum in primary customer growth (+3.5M at that moment), supported by high NPSs. Almost rising from the ashes of the financial crisis,

ING had reclaimed its place, not just as a strong bank but as an incumbent that successfully transformed into a fintech at scale. Restructured and reimagined, we were back where we once were…this time, stronger.

The award was a powerful recognition of the progress we had made. It energized the organization and confirmed our direction was right, but it was not the end of the journey. In many ways, it was only the beginning.

We were in the second phase of our transformation; Accelerated Think Forward had just begun. The foundations were in place, but the deeper organizational shifts were ahead of us. There was still a great deal of work to do.

We had redesigned the bank's infrastructure. At the same time, we were redesigning how 54,000 people worked inside it.

"What I remember most vividly was the pride of our people four or five years into the program, when the outside world started to recognize what we had achieved. Seeing how proud our people were…that's when the spiral really started accelerating, and we moved faster and faster."

—ROEL LOUWHOFF, FORMER ING CHIEF OPERATING
AND CHIEF TRANSFORMATION OFFICER

THE NEW WAY OF WORKING

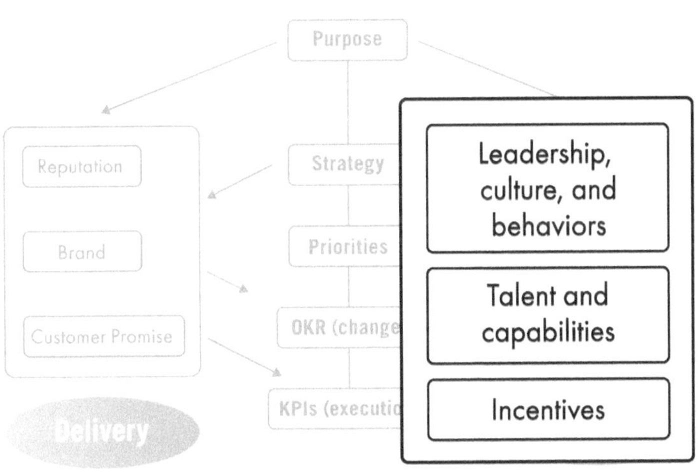

Whenever I traveled to other countries and visited different parts of the organization, I made a habit of frequent floor walks. Whether on a trading floor, a floor with relationship managers, or with our agile teams, I always loved these.

Why? Because it's where I'll find the people who work closest to the customer daily.

I found it fascinating to talk with them about what they were seeing in the market: how well we were doing compared with our competition, also checking on the messages they were receiving from me and the executive team, and what truly landed.

During these floor walks, I consistently noticed the energy in the agile teams. Every morning started with a stand-up meeting (short and focused) to ensure the right level of energy and commitment and to keep communication clear and concise about the day ahead. They were proud to show me how they worked.

If you now ask ten people what "agile" means, you'll get ten different answers. It's become one of those buzzwords, a way of working everyone claims to do, but few understand what it is.

For me, agile is about being clear on the destination while staying flexible on the route to get there. You agree on the purpose, the direction, the outcome, and then you give the team the freedom to decide how best to achieve it.

Agile means flexibility in how you work, how you organize, and how you respond when reality changes. The team owns the route. Leadership sets the ambition and removes obstacles. That combination, clear direction with flexible execution, is what made agile work for us. It is a set of principles, not a way of working per se.

At ING, we didn't adopt agile because it was trendy; it was not really known with incumbents like us. We adopted it because we needed to move faster and fundamentally rethink how we did our work and delivered on our promises. The need for it came directly from our Strategy on a Page: we redefined the role of IT, from a business enabler to the key differentiator in how we do business. On the IT side, agile was already an existing practice (DevOps) at ING since 2011.

Our ambition was to become a digital bank, not just a bank with an app. We needed to become a fully modern organization built around rapid iteration, empowered teams, and real-time customer feedback. That required a completely different operating model, one designed for speed, collaboration, and continuous improvement. With IT much closer to the business, our engineers were now getting direct feedback from customers, enabling faster iteration and more relevant solutions.

THE THINKING BEHIND AGILE

We embraced agile because we needed to operate more like a technology company, moving away from the old waterfall methodology. We didn't call it agile, but we started talking about this way of working on my very first day as CEO. It was one of my key takeaways from that first Silicon Valley trip in 2013.

Traditionally, marketing sees an opportunity to change a product or adjust its interest rate. Product development then develops the product idea around that input. Compliance also contributes. Operations teams design the process through which the product can be delivered. IT starts coding the system based on written requirements.

Once everything is finished, eighteen months may have passed, the money has been spent, and by then, the situation has changed, and the market opportunity may be gone.

This approach works well in a stable and predictable environment. And at the time, banks, including us, were still working in this traditional waterfall model. Big projects. Quarterly releases. Long testing cycles. To operate in a digital world, we needed to move toward something more responsive, something closer to real-time iteration.

To transform into a digital bank, we needed to think like startups and technology companies and move away from the rigid structures of the twentieth century. We needed to fail fast. So we asked: why not shorten the cycle and check progress and viability every two weeks?

That's exactly what we did. To make it work, however, we had to adopt a completely different mindset, one grounded in agile principles. And our new way of working was born.

LEARNING FROM THE DIGITAL NATIVES

Back to my first Silicon Valley trip. When I visited Google, they talked about short time to market, continuous innovation, and real-time testing of new ideas. If you recall, I told you they introduced me to the concept of *pretotyping*: testing new initiatives in real life, getting direct user feedback, and improving continuously. I also shared that they work in multifunctional teams, where businesspeople and software engineers sit together. Amazon called them "two pizza teams." The idea is simple: a team should be large enough to include all the necessary functions but small enough to remain nimble and self-steering, essentially, a group that could share two large American pizzas, about seven to nine people max.

This was exactly the approach we wanted to bring into ING. To deliver on the customer promise, everyone—marketers, product managers, operations staff, and IT engineers—*all* needed to be part of the same team. Not siloed or sequential but working side by side. Not focused on getting it 100 percent right from the beginning but testing or launching at 80 percent and improving from there. Except for specific risk, legal, and compliance requirements.

To develop our new way of working, we took inspiration from the digital natives, companies like Zappos, Spotify, and Google. We studied how they organized their teams, how they connected marketing and engineering, and how they delivered seamless customer experiences through apps and web platforms.

The companies working like this always worked like this, startups that built themselves from scratch with flat, flexible organizations. There were no rigid hierarchies; no one sat around waiting for top-down direction. Everyone contributed. People chased opportunities, tested ideas in real time, and let the results speak for themselves.

"Does this work?"

"Does that feel intuitive?"

"Do customers like it?"

"Let's find out."

They didn't spend months theorizing or relying solely on market research, which often confirms a hypothesis rather than revealing true behavior. They launched, observed, and adjusted. The 80 percent approach.

That mindset, test, learn, adapt, is what inspired us. It's the culture we wanted to emulate. Because if they could move that fast with nothing but an idea, what could we do with our scale and resources, if we worked the same way?

But since no other incumbent had tried it, we could not learn from their mistakes. We had to go first.

Here's how we did it.

THE TESTING GROUND

Agile wasn't something we bolted on. It was a behavioral, cultural, and structural redesign, and it changed everything.

ING Netherlands became our pilot ground, where its leaders started years earlier to transform a 10,000-person organization.[7]

Before we could run fast, we had to clean house. That started with redesigning our customer journeys and reducing the number of products and processes across ING Netherlands.

They created "washing lanes" where marketers, product owners, and IT came together (without their managers) to clean up legacy processes and products. They simplified from 2,000 to 400 processes, eliminating redundancy, waste, and confusion.

It wasn't glamorous work, but it was essential groundwork. They didn't just adopt agile. They cleared the path for it first.

They started from a traditional, hierarchical, and bureaucratic structure, divided into vertical silos like marketing, product management, operations, and technology. The challenge was: How to cut across *all* of that? How to shift from vertical to horizontal and create small, cross-functional teams that are highly flexible in what they do? When should risk management and compliance participate in such teams at the appropriate stage of the development process, whether for a proposition, process, or product?

They also had to rethink management, restructure the layers, and deliberately remove traditional managerial roles. The goal was to reduce hierarchy, eliminate bureaucracy, and force empowerment so decisions could be made quickly, even for small changes.

These multifunctional teams should do, in two-week sprints, what used to take months. They were to be responsible for everything: from shaping the customer proposition to engineering the actual experience. Because true innovation lives in the day-to-day decisions made at the working level. The best people belong on the frontlines. They know how things really work, understand what our customers want, and see how customers respond to new features in the app. That customer feedback loop is immediate and crucial. If something works, they keep it. If it doesn't, they kill it.

This is the foundation of agile.

"We were building a house, but we put all the plumbers in one building, all the carpenters in another, all the electricians in a third. Agile meant flipping that completely. In an agile world, you bring one or two plumbers, one or two carpenters, one or two electricians to the site. They arrive together. They take off their jackets. They go to work. They deliver. That, to me, is agile: putting people from different disciplines in the same team, from day one, to deliver what the customer actually wants."

—PAYAM DJAVDAN, FORMER ING GLOBAL HEAD OF
OPERATING MODEL AND WAY OF WORKING

At ING Netherlands, we reorganized 3,500 employees, 2,500 from IT and 1,000 from business, into 350 multidisciplinary squads of no more than nine people. Indeed, not everyone had a place in the new organization. On June 15, 2015, ING Netherlands launched this new model in the Ajax stadium in Amsterdam. It was fast, it was radical, and it set the foundation for everything that followed. In the end, the results of agile spoke for itself. Sixty percent of squads were able to ship to production within just two sprints, drastically improving time to market. In the Netherlands, we achieved a 33 percent efficiency gain, exceeding our original targets. Most importantly, employee engagement soared to 90 percent, proving that when people are empowered, they don't just perform better; they show up with energy and purpose.

WHAT IT TOOK TO BUILD AGILE-READY TECH

We couldn't bolt agile onto a legacy system. That meant:

- Moving from quarterly to biweekly release cycles
- Enabling squads to own end-to-end delivery
- Shifting from siloed platforms to shared environments
- Empowering teams with real-time data and rapid testing tools

We had to rebuild the machine.

Before ING's agile transformation, the bank's technology systems were only structured for control and coordination, not also for speed or autonomy. Most technology operated in large, centralized monoliths that required extensive planning, long testing cycles, and multiple layers of sign-off. Delivery was slow, because every release had dependencies, across teams, across departments, and often across entire business units.

Like we covered in the previous chapter, to enable agile, the technology platform had to be re-architected to support:

- Continuous Integration/Continuous Deployment (CI/CD): code could move from testing to production without a massive release train.
- Decoupled services: one squad's feature didn't depend on another squad's timeline.
- Shared infrastructure and visibility: customer support, engineering, and operations were all working from the same data and systems.
- Lightweight, visual tooling: teams could collaborate in real time and track progress without delays.

This required more than just installing new tools. It meant breaking apart the legacy systems into modular components and creating a technical foundation where autonomous squads could ship product on their own...and they did.

These teams needed to replan every two weeks, adapt continuously to customer feedback, and operate with real autonomy. Yes, they were part of a larger strategic direction set at the top, but within that broader plan, they were the ones steering the change.

DECIDING ON MULTIFUNCTIONAL TEAMS

We built agile around multifunctional, self-steering teams.

To support this shift, we brought in agile coaches to help teams learn and practice this new way of working, and we restructured the organization around tribes, chapters, and squads. Squads were small, cross-functional teams with end-to-end responsibility for a specific customer outcome or problem. Tribes grouped related squads together around a broader mission, creating scale without losing autonomy. Chapters connected people with similar skills, such as engineering, data, or design, across squads, ensuring professional standards, knowledge sharing, and development. This structure replaced traditional hierarchies with a system designed for speed, clarity, and accountability while keeping expertise strong and coordination tight across the organization.

Squad

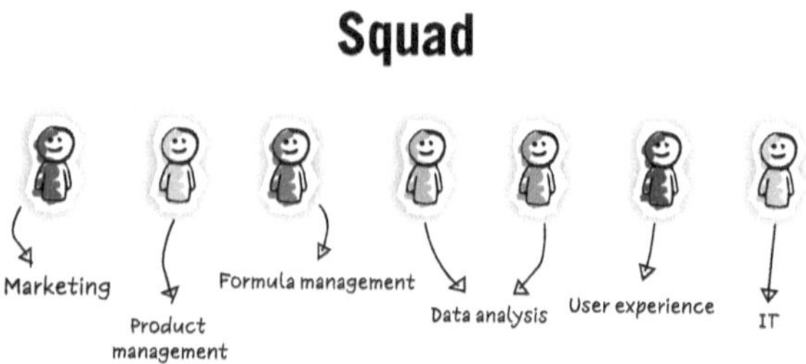

A typical squad might include a marketer, a product manager, data analyst, UX specialist, someone from channels, and a couple of engineers. These teams were small, usually no more than nine people, and self-steering by design. There was no *formal* leader (there *was* oversight, which I'll explain further on). Everyone was expected to know enough to contribute across disciplines.

They operated on a rhythm:

- Daily standups to check progress
- Biweekly planning meetings to recalibrate
- A new assignment every quarter

Someone might say, "I think we should approach it this way," and others would weigh in, collaborating, adjusting, and moving quickly.

Visual tools were key. Flip charts, sticky notes (later, digital boards), anything that made progress visible. Teams gathered standing up, often nine people at a time, for short, focused meetings where everyone was expected to pay attention. One person would take the lead and quickly run through the essentials: *What did you achieve yesterday? What's your plan for today? Where do we need to coordinate?*

Every two weeks, they reviewed commitments together:

- What did we say we'd deliver?
- Did we do it?
- If not, why not?

The energy in those moments was unmistakable. You'd see people stepping forward who were far less senior, with no formal authority, taking responsibility for the day's work. No one was waiting to be told what to do. If something wasn't working, the answer was simple: fail fast, try something else. No hierarchy. Just fast, empowered, self-organizing teams and a level of ownership and momentum that was incredible to watch.

Failing fast was the way to progress and learn. However, in risk and compliance aspects, there was zero tolerance to fail fast.

FINDING THE RIGHT WAY TO DEVELOP TALENT

In our self-steering teams, there was always some form of oversight, typically a product owner assigned for a three-month period. They observed the team's progress and provided quarterly feedback, alongside the chapter leads and agile coaches.

However, that also meant someone could have up to four different product owners in a year. They weren't working under a single "boss." Instead, they received input from multiple perspectives: the product owner on *what* they did, chapter lead on *how* they did their work, and agile coaches on their *collaboration* culture. It created a rotating peer review that helped people grow.

Otherwise...

- How do you ensure that self-steering teams steer themselves?
- What do you do if someone doesn't show up?
- If they do, how do you ensure they deliver?
- How do you give praise, and how do you develop talent in this model?

It's a mind-bender. The theory is elegant, but the implementation is tough.

A lot of our early focus was on dismantling old structures. This is the other side: how do you *build* the new one?

We had already brought in agile coaches to guide people through it, but what we needed went deeper than coaching. Finding the right talent was one of the core challenges. It's one of the reasons why agile succeeds or fails. If we didn't get this part right, the rest wouldn't work.

Two Critical Characteristics: Collaboration and Accountability

There were two major characteristics we looked for in people working within the agile model.

The first was collaboration. You had to be highly cooperative, because you weren't working in isolation. You were working across many functions to get things done. People who stayed in their own lane, focused only on their role or responsibilities, didn't have the right mindset. They weren't the right leaders for an agile organization.

The second was accountability. Specifically, a willingness to accept the responsibility that comes with empowered decision-making.

Everyone says, "I want to make decisions by myself."

So we'd say, "Okay, here you go. Make them. But we're going to hold you accountable for the results."

The leaders we needed were those who could both collaborate across teams and fully own their decisions.

ELIMINATING TITLES, ELEVATING VOICES

Getting rid of titles might not sound revolutionary, unless you've worked in banking.

In this industry, titles are everything. We identify ourselves with our titles: Vice President, Director, Managing Director. Titles are how people measure status. Promotions mean prestige, and prestige is tied to hierarchy.

We wanted to change that. Titles reinforced old power structures, the kind that slow organizations down, silence good ideas, and make people wait their turn to speak. In an agile world, that's a liability. What we needed was a culture that prioritized contribution over hierarchy, substance over seniority. Like we had done with the Leadership Council.

So we got rid of titles.

It was a bold move, especially for those who had spent ten or fifteen years climbing the corporate ladder. For many, titles were a source of hard-earned pride. The shift wasn't about stripping away value, though. It was about refocusing it. You weren't the "Managing Director, Head of Call Centers" anymore. You were the client service lead or a client service specialist, a title that described your role, not your rank or function.

The message was clear: what matters is what you bring to the table, not where you sit on the org chart. Everyone has a voice. And anyone, no matter how junior, can raise a hand, challenge an idea, or lead a conversation. Leadership became something you demonstrated, not something you inherited through promotions.

A CULTURAL MIRROR TO AGILE

While the agile transformation was underway at ING Netherlands, we were also developing the Orange Code.

The Orange Code was born from intuition and values, not methodology. But as the new way of working progressed at ING Netherlands, we started noticing something striking: the behaviors that made agile work were the same ones we were codifying in the Orange Code as a derivative from the purpose.

They weren't designed together, and yet, they aligned perfectly. Striking? Maybe not. Both emerged as necessary responses to a changing culture and new ways of working, each developed with the Strategy on a Page in mind.

Agile called for autonomous teams, empowered individuals, and proactive collaboration. So did the Orange Code. One emerged from a shift in ways of working, the other from a shift in mindset, but they both pointed to the same core truth.

I remember Hein saying once, "The Orange Code has nothing to do with agile."

I disagreed. I said, "It has everything to do with agile."

So it wasn't that we built the Orange Code specifically to support working with agile principles, but both emerged from the same foundation: a deep assessment of who we were and who we needed to become to deliver on our strategy. It captured the values and behaviors already present in the organization, along with those essential for the future.

When the new way of working was being rolled out, particularly with the Dutch teams, we connected just in time to align the two efforts. It made perfect sense. The Orange Code and the agile principles in our way of working reinforced each other, giving cultural clarity to a new way of operating.

THE NETHERLANDS: ING'S AGILE PROTOTYPE

For a legacy institution like ING, adopting agile was more than a new way of working. We were used to formal handovers, strict project timelines, and rigid testing cycles. The shift to empowered teams and iterative delivery felt radical.

That's why the transformation in the Netherlands, between 2014 and 2016, was so pivotal. ING Netherlands became the first part of the organization to fully implement the agile principles at scale. It was our live experiment, the prototype for what agile could look like in banking. They made mistakes, but more importantly, they tested new team structures, ran real-time experiments, and redefined how we selected people, not just for skills but for mindset. Their courage gave the rest of ING a working model to learn from.

To limit the risk of implementation, at this stage, we deliberately excluded areas like risk management and compliance from the transformation.

DELIVERY VS. SERVICE

The initial transformation focused on the delivery organization: the part of the business responsible for making continuous improvements, or even better: innovations. That included streamlining processes, updating the app, modifying product conditions, and deploying new technology. In that context, agile worked well. It allowed multidisciplinary teams to move quickly, make decisions locally, and ship improvements regularly.

Later, we tried to apply agile principles to the way of working in the service organization, the teams responsible for day-to-day client interactions. This wasn't about changing the product or system. It was about how we showed up for customers in real time.

In branches, for example, we experimented with replacing the traditional structure of mortgage specialists, payment specialists, and managers. Instead, we introduced a flat, self-steering team, where anyone could assist any client, and the team set its own targets. We tried the same approach in call centers.

The results weren't the same.

Agile thrived in delivery, where teams were solving problems, building solutions, and iterating on improvements after customer feedback. In service, it proved far harder to implement. Being able to service a customer regardless of your specialist background was complex and often bound by compliance. The rhythm was different. The handoffs weren't as easily removed. The mindset shift didn't translate as cleanly in getting the right answer or advice for the customer.

THE GLOBAL AGILE ROLLOUT

Once we saw that agile was working well in the delivery organization in the Netherlands, we began rolling it out globally. The international roll out clearly highlighted cultural differences in the countries. Many were enthusiastic to embrace and implement it, but for example in Germany the employee satisfaction dropped. This was the only country where that happened. People at first felt less comfortable with autonomy and working with a product backlog instead of well-specified program milestones (waterfall). Over time that changed.

The second goal was to ensure that every country organized its teams the same way.

That meant our tribes, chapters, and squads had to be structured consistently across the entire organization. If we could standardize the model, we could also share talent and resources across markets. Germany could help the Netherlands, Belgium could help Romania, Spain could help Italy, etc.

If each country was organized differently, that kind of collaboration wouldn't be possible. We wouldn't be able to reallocate capacity or prioritize across borders. If we couldn't do that, we wouldn't truly be one organization.

That was the next big step: we standardized both the organizational structure and the way of working across all countries. As we described in Chapter 6: The Blueprint of a Digital Bank, we also centralized the management of capacity and cost for that part of the business, €1 billion a year, and decided the allocation in the QBRs.

WHOLESALE BANKING: AGILE BY ANOTHER NAME

Wholesale banking was, and wasn't, already working with agile principles. From a technology and delivery perspective, it was ahead. By design, the wholesale organization operated globally. With clients in more than forty countries, there was no way to build bespoke systems for each jurisdiction. The engineering stack had to be shared. Infrastructure, payments, cash management, trade finance, these are inherently cross-border services governed by international regulations and consistent contractual structures. Standardization wasn't an ambition. It was a necessity.

That gave wholesale a major advantage. While the retail side of the business at that time was still operating largely at the country level, wholesale had already adopted the kind of centralized, scalable approach we were working to implement elsewhere. Prioritizing global capacity and delivering from shared systems wasn't a transformation; it was business as usual.

Culturally, however, wholesale was more traditional. Agile, as a term, didn't land. When we introduced it, many leaders there said, "That's not really for us."

I'd reply, "But you're already doing it."

Think about how the wholesale model works: a relationship manager knows the client deeply but delivers value by collaborating with internal specialists, cash management, lending, DCM, ECM, M&A, and more. Those specialists operate as a single cross-functional team. That's a squad. That's agile.

Wholesale had been doing it all along. They just weren't using the same vocabulary. The way they solved problems, fluid, cross-silo, solution-first, was a direct match with agile principles.

The resistance wasn't to the model. It was to the *label*.

But the label helped put words to what they were already doing well. That mattered, because as the structure existed, naming it helped us scale it. It gave us a shared language to connect practices across the business and move the rest of the organization toward a more global, integrated, and agile way of working.

WHAT WE LEARNED

"Agile was a perfect solution, brilliantly chosen, for a specific business challenge. But then we overdid it. We confused means and ends. Agile was never meant to be applied everywhere, to every part of the bank. That's what happens in large organizations. We find something that works, and then we apply it blindly. We then learned and corrected."

—HEIN KNAAPEN, FORMER ING HEAD OF HR

People often expect that working with agile principles is to drive more innovation. But the productivity and customer experience improvement sits in dealing with the product backlogs that encourages people to focus on their current goals and products. The motivation comes from receiving customer feedback directly and being able, in the multi-functional team, to quickly deliver on this.

Some inside ING believed the ambition of converting the company to agile was never fully realized. It was a powerful vision, bold, future-oriented, and widely embraced in principle but difficult to implement in full.

Those close to the transformation saw it differently. From their perspective, the transition from waterfall to agile was successful and transformative in itself. The technical foundation held. The structures endured. The underlying philosophy reshaped how people worked, even if it didn't look exactly like the original blueprint.

Both perspectives are true. Agile wasn't one moment or outcome; it was a cultural reckoning, a systems overhaul, and a leadership challenge rolled into one. And where the introduction failed, we needed to adapt. That is what agile is about after all.

Be agile with agile.

After the initial implementation of a new way of working, you need to maintain *and* improve the operating model. You have to be agile with agile…otherwise in the end everything deteriorates and enthusiasm fades.

The introduction of cross-border orchestration helped drive the consistency in our transformation. It ensured the priorities and standards were set consistently across the business, and it specifically helped in areas of risk management and compliance with new pan-European directives in AML and laws like MiFID II and GDPR.

Central capacity planning, however, created a bottleneck. Teams had to justify their projects, explain their priorities, and report upward. That process started to drag, whereas the benefit of moving tech capacity across divisions and countries was limited.

Over time, we became incrementally more successful in delivering what we wanted.

Our original vision was one brand, one experience, one app, and shared and standardized tech across borders, with the product elements that were delivered staying local. Most of this was delivered.

Sharing and standardization of the tech stack, risk management, data management, and compliance management worked, but parts had to stay local, though. National supervisors did not support full cross-border integration.

To use an analogy: Facebook's platform and user experience is the same around the world, but the content you see depends on local rules. The same was true for us. The customer interface, data management, algorithms (read risk models) could (largely) be standardized, but the underlying financial products were shaped by national regulation. That limited our ability to gain efficiencies from standardization in that part.

When we designed the strategy, we believed the European Banking Union would materialize in full. That was the entire premise behind the creation of the Single Supervisory Mechanism (SSM) to unify regulatory frameworks and enable true cross-border banking. The Banking Union officially launched on October 1, 2014, just as we were beginning this transformation.

In mid-2020, as I was stepping down to become CEO of UBS, it was clear the promise of the Banking Union hadn't been fulfilled. Local regulators held tight control over local parts of ING, with European rules and laws always implemented with a local tweak. COVID-19 made it even worse, because during the pandemic, local regulators and governments tightened their grip on the use of the balance sheet, prioritizing national economies over European integration.

After I left, in the retail bank ING had to find a new balance, keeping a consistent digital experience and brand while keeping product development and delivery local. Several of the smaller markets weren't profitable on their own. Countries like the Czech Republic and Austria could only succeed by fully leveraging shared systems, products, and standardized processes. When some of that became impossible, ING decided to divest. Regulators wouldn't align, and profitability remained out of reach because of a low-rate environment, so those countries had to stand on their own or go.

That's the reality of execution. The environment shifts, and leadership must respond. Most of the ideas we introduced held strong. Some couldn't continue, not because they were wrong but because the context changed. And a few? A few didn't work.

But one thing never changed: I would never go back to waterfall.

Projects get too big. They take too long. They drift too far from the customer. They become buried in bureaucracy. Waterfall slows down the very thing we were trying to do: deliver better experiences for the people we serve.

Agile at ING wasn't a checklist or a consultant-led reorg. It was a fundamental shift in how we worked, how we led, and how we delivered value. Real agility doesn't come from ceremonies or sticky notes. It comes from trust. From leaders recognizing they can't decide on everything. From teams empowered to act. From cultures built on transparency, collaboration, and shared goals. Agile helped us move faster and move together.

It was never about chasing a buzzword; we were the first incumbent to use it. It was about reshaping the way we worked, how we organized teams, built technology, and made decisions to move at the speed our customers expected. The shift was bold, sometimes messy, or misunderstood, but it proved that a bank could think and act like a digital native. Still, designing a new operating model was only half the story. To make it stick, leaders had to let go of old habits and guide their people through uncertainty and change.

Our colleagues at ING can be proud that we were a first mover in introducing agile as an incumbent. It helped us lead and move faster. Many other established organizations, banks, and beyond visited us and were inspired by the energy it unleashed and the speed it enabled. Most went on to replicate our model, some more than others.

Agile reshaped our behaviors. We also needed to make those behaviors visible and tangible.

CHAPTER 8

ING'S CAMPUS

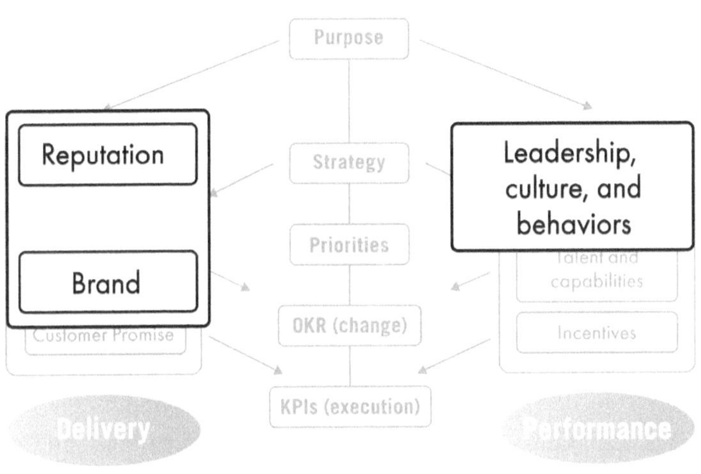

ING's campus was the physical manifestation of our strategy and culture. We designed it to reinforce openness, collaboration, and empowerment, embedding our purpose and agile way of working into the daily experience of coming to work. The building itself shaped behavior, accelerated connection, and signaled who we were becoming.

When I stepped foot onto the Google Campus, I was mesmerized. It was during my Silicon Valley visit, right before my CEO tenure. I saw different buildings in a park-like environment, open-floor seating for everyone in the organization, designated areas for socialization or rest, and people collaborating. I knew, in that moment, that if ING was to fully become a digital bank, we needed a campus.

In 2013, our physical environment reflected the old world: hierarchical, closed off, and disconnected. Traditional *vertical* office buildings, where people ride an elevator to their floor and stay siloed, don't empower employees to do their best work. They don't build a shared identity. People might collaborate with their direct team, go down for lunch, then disappear again, never seeing the rest of the business.

How could we expect to embed the purpose into ING's culture if the working environment doesn't reflect it?

We needed something different. We needed buildings with large open floors that we could access via stairs, rather than elevators, so colleagues would engage and collaborate. We needed several horizontal buildings, close together, where people could walk to and meet their colleagues.

It would help rebuild the social tissue, connect people not just to their teams but to a shared purpose and vision.

We couldn't build the campus overnight, however; we needed to start incrementally where we currently were. Toward the end of 2014 and into 2015, I asked everyone on the executive team to move to the same floor. We made smaller open rooms and glass walls. I believed it would improve our communication and empower transformation. Empowerment isn't just a slogan; it shows up in the environment you create. This was a first step; there was only so much we could do in the building we were in.

It was the beginning of the changes to ING's environment.

Our Think Forward strategy was already pointing us in a clear direction: a more transparent, accessible, tech-driven bank. Strategy alone was not enough. The environment had to reflect the ambition. A place that made our purpose, "empowering people to stay a step ahead in life and in business," tangible in the day-to-day experience of coming to work. As Nanne Bos's team articulated, architecture and interior design aren't cosmetic; they can shape behavior. A good workspace "plugs into culture," and a great one "amplifies it."

The impetus for the campus was simple but fundamental: if we wanted to transform the bank, we needed a setting that supported the transformation. A place where:

- Leadership wouldn't be hidden on executive floors but part of the flow of daily life.
- Teams could move, collaborate, and innovate freely.
- Our purpose and our culture weren't abstract ideas but something people could feel physically the moment they walked in the door.

The campus wasn't an architectural project; it was an identity project. A symbolic break from the post-crisis years and a physical manifestation of the organization we were choosing to build next.

BEFORE THE CAMPUS

Before we built the campus, our office landscape reflected exactly where ING was at that moment in time: fragmented. We were spread across multiple sites, including the old headquarters in the iconic but inward-facing building called "The Sandcastle," designed by Alberts & Van Huut. It was a beautiful piece of architecture, but the interior made it difficult for people to truly connect with one another because of its compartmentalized structure and closed circulation patterns.

Teams were physically separated, often by department or business line, and people largely stayed in their own zones, floors, and towers. Leadership was physically separated, reinforcing the hierarchy of the past. It mirrored a style of working that had grown up over decades, one that favored long meetings in meeting rooms, sequential decision-making, and strictly defined organizational boundaries. The building was perfectly suited to the ING of the past and poorly suited to the ING we needed to become.

The physical environment amplified our organizational challenges. When teams sit in silos, they behave in silos. The distance between functions slowed decision-making, the limited visibility across departments made collaboration more difficult, and the lack of shared spaces meant the energy of the organization was diffused instead of concentrated. Even our seating reflected old logic: you sat with your department, not with the people you needed to solve problems with. People would communicate through email with colleagues one floor down rather than get up and walk there. This kind of layout encourages "acting together for common benefit" but not true collaboration, because proximity isn't the same as interaction.

In that environment, it was nearly impossible to create the sense of unity and momentum we were striving for with Think Forward. We needed a place where people could see and feel each other's work, where leaders were naturally part of the flow rather than hidden behind executive corridors, and where cross-functional teams could form organically, move quickly, and share knowledge in real time.

THE CAMPUS LOCATION

ING's buildings were spread around in a specific area of Amsterdam, and I wanted to ensure all ING colleagues would work in buildings that were very close. A real campus, with green space in between, colleagues walking from one building to another, with a nice place to have coffee, lunch, and after-work drinks at the center.

If we wanted to facilitate new behavior, collaboration, and innovation, if we wanted to encourage the behaviors we defined in our Orange Code, we needed to translate that into our campus and office design. The campus project brought culture, identity, and brand together in a physical space.

The campus development started in my first year as CEO, and the first two buildings were completed just four months before I announced my move to UBS. The campus became a red thread running through every aspect of our transformation.

I remember speaking with the mayor of Amsterdam at the time, Mr. Eberhard van der Laan. When we were discussing our new location, most banks and large companies were moving to Amsterdam Zuidas. We felt strongly that we should stay where we were: in a part of the city with more social and cultural diversity. We wanted to make a statement of commitment to the Bijlmer, in Amsterdam-Zuidoost.

The mayor, a devoted Ajax fan, attended matches every other week. On his way to the stadium, he always passed what he called "one of the ugliest buildings in Amsterdam." He said to me, "Ralph, if you can do something about that, I'll come and open the campus when it's finished."

So we did. That building was located exactly where we wanted to be, at the center of several ING buildings that were there already. We tore down that old building, remediated the asbestos, and reused the concrete for the new foundation. We built the center of the campus right there on that site, so people could easily walk from one ING building to another.

Although the mayor couldn't attend the opening, he made it a point to join me in planting the first tree. He was terminally ill at the time but still came. We were grateful for his passion to develop this part of Amsterdam, just like his successor, who opened the campus.

DESIGNING THE CAMPUS

The design process itself was deeply collaborative. Real estate, branding, facilities, the architecture teams, and my leadership group were all involved. There were design workshops, internal reviews, and iterative sessions to ensure that the new building reflected the brand and the culture we were building. Space can reinforce the Orange Code by shaping behavior, so every design choice needed to align with who we wanted to be as an organization.

A LIVING METAPHOR

When we committed to building the new campus, I never saw it as "just" a headquarters project. The central building (called Cedar) had a job to do. It needed to enable the bank we were becoming: customer-centric, built around empowered teams, and digital-first. Our strategy required speed and integration, and I wanted a physical environment that made those ways of working natural, intuitive, and inevitable. In my view, Cedar needed to be as horizontal as possible, not vertical. Horizontal buildings make people walk to each other; in vertical buildings people stay on their floor and lose time taking elevators.

For us, digital was the operating model. We were moving toward platform-based banking, with engineers and business teams working side by side to deliver new customer experiences at pace. The building needed to support that shift by giving people a place where they could collaborate easily, test and learn quickly, and make decisions without the friction of bureaucracy or geography.

Equally important, the building needed to hardwire our agile transformation. We were organizing around chapters, tribes, and squads, and we needed spaces that supported those rituals: stand-ups, informal huddles, retrospectives, and spontaneous collaboration. Inspired by the changes ING Netherlands introduced in the Acanthus building on the campus, Cedar was to be designed for agile with an open and flexible floor plan and a way of physically connecting people and ideas.

To support rapid iteration and flexible team formation, entire areas of the building were reimagined around three modes of work: collaborate, concentrate, and congregate.

Need quiet focus for half an hour? Move to a concentration zone. Working through a sprint backlog with your squad? Head to the collaboration space. Want to reflect, reset, or ping-pong an idea? That's what the congregate areas were for.

The campus was also an opportunity to reinforce our purpose and brand in ways that were authentic, not superficial. Our purpose gave people freedom, choice, accessibility, and intuitive navigation. Those values were emphasized by the location of Cedar: at the center of the campus. Benthem Crouwel, the exterior architects, proposed to create a setback and a large green space in front of Cedar. It symbolized accessibility and transparency, qualities we wanted customers and employees to feel immediately when they walked on the campus and approached the building. The horizontal, transparent exterior architecture of Cedar signaled openness and modernity, a deliberate contrast to the more closed and hierarchical atmosphere of our old headquarters.

These values were also physically embedded in Cedar: from the open atrium to the ease of movement, to the visibility across floors, to the presence of greenery and natural light. The interior architects made sure these qualities were not decorative but structural. They went even further: Michiel Hofman of HofmanDujardin, translated the concept of digital platforms into actual physical platforms: three-dimensional spaces, bridges, and stairs that encouraged people to move through the building and meet one another naturally.

Leadership transformation was another key objective. We wanted to replace hierarchy with accessibility. In the old building, leaders had a separate entrance. In Cedar, that separation disappeared. Private offices also disappeared. The executive team set the example by working in open space, and we were intentionally placed in the center of Cedar, not on the top floor, so employees naturally encountered us on the platforms, stairs, and open areas. We chose to sit on a long table, where we could do our work like anyone else. For specific meetings we would use offices we needed to reserve. It was a deliberate move to support the culture we were trying to build: accessible, open, and nonhierarchical.

The shift from private offices to shared, flexible spaces was one of the biggest transformations embedded in the design. We introduced unassigned desks, communal areas, and co-creation rooms designed for multidisciplinary squads. Of course, this shift didn't happen without internal debate. Giving up private offices was not easy for everyone. Many felt their seniority entitled them to having their own office, like a status symbol. But since the executive team worked at a large table, there was no excuse. Also moving to flexible spaces (and the idea that you might sit somewhere different each day) felt uncomfortable at first. People asked practical questions:

- Where do I put my things?
- How do I focus?
- What happens to team identity if we don't sit together?

These were fair concerns, and we spent time addressing them through the design itself. We introduced a mix of open collaboration zones, project rooms, private focus spaces, and informal meeting areas so that employees could choose the environment that best supported their work during the day.

Walls of any kind around large departments or offices weren't allowed. Suddenly, many departments needing to move out of the old building felt they could do without the earlier excuse of confidentiality as everyone wanted to move to the new building. Larger departments that really needed to be separate for true confidentiality or regulatory reasons would move to other buildings on the campus to facilitate this, only a short walk away from Cedar.

Despite the early resistance, the design ultimately spoke for itself. The glass walls made activity visible; the communal spaces created energy and flow; the co-creation rooms enabled real-time collaboration; the platforms encouraged movement and chance encounters.

AN OPEN CAMPUS

Finally, the campus was designed to become an ecosystem. I wanted it to be more than a workplace, a place where employees, partners, startups, students, regulators, and even the surrounding community could come together. Early concepts even explored hosting public cultural events, performances, and gatherings in the atrium, reinforcing ING's connection to society and the idea that empowerment extends beyond our own people.

To foster the idea that innovation happens where creative people meet, we developed the concept of opening the campus up for third parties. We called it Cumulus Park. The idea was to attract the best engineers to support the bank in making technology a differentiator. Since most engineers are inherently creative, they might be excited to build something, to contribute to a compelling vision, but at some point, they'll likely have their own bright idea. When they do, they'll want to go out, start a company, and build it themselves.

That's part of their DNA, and we had to accept that. In fact, we had to design for it.

So we built a space on campus specifically for entrepreneurial exploration. We dedicated two floors of Cedar to it. Technically outside the bank's formal structure but supported by us, these floors offered engineers workspace, access to technology, and the chance to pursue their own ideas. They could experiment. They could build their own startup. They could take risks. Outside of the bank but on our campus.

If they failed? They could come back.

That was the beauty of it. Failure wasn't a mark against them; it was part of the journey. A failed startup didn't make them less valuable. It made them more experienced, more capable. We would welcome them back as better engineers than before. By giving them the freedom to try, we also deepened their loyalty. They knew we believed in them, not just as employees but as builders, creators, and future founders.

IMPACT AND SUSTAINABILITY

As mentioned, the exterior architects deliberately incorporated a setback and green landscape, integrating nature into the campus and creating an accessible, welcoming environment. The large park-like space in front of Cedar and the extensive use of greenery indoors reflected a commitment to wellbeing and a connection to nature, principles that align with contemporary sustainability practices and employee health. The park, albeit privately owned, is open to the public for people to enjoy.

Of course, given our ambition in sustainability, it was important for Cedar to achieve the highest possible sustainability rating, BREEAM-NL Outstanding, with an overall score of 93.7 percent. At the time, this was the top rating awarded by the renowned sustainability rater BREEAM-NL, based on scores across nine categories, including health, energy, transportation, and waste.

BRAND: ORANGE MADE TANGIBLE

One of the most meaningful outcomes of the campus was the way it expressed our brand without relying on logos. As the architects explained, you could "read and feel the brand" through the setup of the campus, but also the space in Cedar itself: the openness, the transparency, the freedom of movement, and the sense of possibility when you enter the atrium.

Where tech companies use interior design to express identity, we did the same. Visual cues, light, greenery, open lines of sight, intuitive navigation, and touches of color created an atmosphere that reflected optimism, simplicity, and forward momentum.

OPENING: A NEW ERA FOR ING

The opening of the campus in 2019 marked a turning point for ING. After years of development, design reviews, construction phases, and countless decisions that shaped everything from the architecture to the smallest interior detail, seeing people walking across the campus and entering into Cedar for the first time was extraordinary.

One of the first things that happened that day was completely unplanned: a fire alarm. Not everything in the new building was fully ready yet, and the alarm went off shortly after people arrived. Technically, everyone should have exited using the fire stairs, but instead, instinctively, people gathered on the platforms in the atrium, the very heart of the building, exactly as the architects had envisioned. It was striking to see how quickly those platforms became the natural gathering place, even in an unexpected moment. To me, it showed how intuitive the space was. People gravitated to the place that felt communal.

I gave my first speech in the new building standing on the staircase. (I'll tell you what I introduced in that speech in the next chapter about branding.) Delivering that message from the steps felt intentional, even if I hadn't planned it that way. The staircase had always symbolized openness and movement, and now it became the stage for a new chapter in our culture.

"When I watched Ralph give that first speech from the staircase, it struck me how perfectly it embodied what we set out to build. Seeing people gather on the steps, the platforms, and the bridges above showed the architecture working exactly as intended. It created connectivity, a shared sense of purpose, and a feeling of meeting one another openly in this new environment we had imagined."

—MICHIEL HOFMAN, ING CAMPUS LEAD INTERIOR ARCHITECT

You could feel the shift in the building immediately after that first gathering. People moved differently through the space. They paused on the landings, talked across levels, and explored corners with a mix of curiosity and excitement. Teams walked the atrium, climbed the stairs, crossed the bridges: exactly as we had envisioned.

For the organization, the message was unmistakable: we weren't just entering a new building; we were entering a new era. The campus signaled, to our people and to the outside world, that ING was no longer a bank rebuilding after the crisis. We were a bank that had reinvented itself.

THE CAMPUS TODAY

Two months after we opened the campus and Cedar, it needed to be reconfigured for social distancing. COVID-19, with waves of lockdowns, minimized the use of the buildings temporarily. Also, Cumulus Park, the open campus meant to attract startup talent, did not take off. After the lockdowns, new startups worked from home, and the need for support by ING was not there anymore.

More recently, the openness of the campus buildings has been frequently vandalized by activists. ING built security barriers immediately after entering the building. How ironic.

But. (There is always a but.)

When I look at the campus today, what strikes me most is how naturally it continues to reflect the transformation we set out to achieve. With Cedar at the center, and the Maple building redesigned, the campus connects two other buildings, Acanthus and the building hosting ING's trading floor. Next to Cedar, a new building is being built, which will complete the campus.

The campus remains a central gathering place for leadership

and teams. The original design choices continue to influence how people work and connect. People gather naturally. Leaders remain accessible. Teams move easily across disciplines. The design still shapes behavior in quiet but powerful ways.

For me, the most important thing is that the campus continues to symbolize what ING is: a digital bank that puts customers at the core. It remains a space that mirrors ING's purpose and amplifies the Orange Code behaviors.

The campus idea was not to create a headquarters.

It was a commitment to a different way of working, a different kind of culture, and a different vision for the bank.

Today, it remains living proof of that transformation. It was never about architecture. It was about identity. It made our strategy physical, our culture visible, and our ambition unmistakable, and it became the natural stage for the moment when everything we had been building finally found its voice.

CHAPTER 9

LIVING THE BRAND

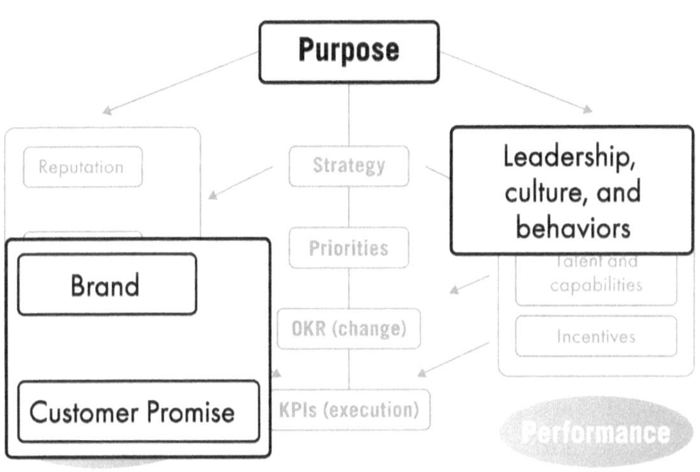

Brand at ING became our alignment mechanism, and the launch of Do Your Thing was the moment our brand caught up with our reality. After years of hard work in strategy, simplification, digitalization, culture, and shared ways of working, we were ready to make a customer promise that matched the experience.

It was a cold January morning.

The kind of cold that sharpens everything: the air, the light, the quiet before a crowd moves. I remember walking downstairs, not rushing, just letting the moment arrive. Outside, hundreds of colleagues were already gathering. Orange beanies everywhere. A sea of people standing together in the cold, waiting.

Through its glass windows, ING's new campus reflected back at us. It was clean, modern, deliberate.

On the outside of those windows, a familiar shape appeared first. The orange ING app icon: the cropped lion's head. Instantly recognizable, even from a distance.

And just beneath it, in the same orange, the words:

Do Your Thing.

Not projected. Not announced on a screen. Just a decal in the windows: quiet, confident, unmistakable. The digital symbol people carried in their pockets, paired with the promise we were finally ready to make out loud.

Seven years.

That's how long it had taken to get here. Seven years of work that didn't always look like brand work. Years spent fixing foundations, simplifying systems, rebuilding trust, and earning the right to say something meaningful. Years where we resisted the temptation to announce before we were ready.

Because a brand promise only matters if you can live up to it.

Standing there that morning in the cold with thousands of colleagues, looking at those words on the glass, it finally came together. All of it. Every decision, every debate, every iteration collapsed into three words.

Do Your Thing.

That was the moment. Not when the words were written. Not when the logo was finalized. But when the promise became visible and grounded in the work we had already done and the behavior we expected from ourselves going forward.

This was not a marketing line. It was a description of how we expected clients and colleagues to experience us. Freedom. Confidence. The ability to move through life without friction and focus on what matters.

ONE COMPANY, ONE BRAND?

Back to 2013. The whiteboard stretched across the wall, covered edge to edge with eighty-four different ING payment cards. Different colors. Different layouts. Different lions. Some barely recognizable as ING at all.

Nanne had pinned up every active card design he could find. Eighty-four different cards.

I stood there for a moment, taking it in.

I shook my head. "This is one company."

"Yes," he said. "But not one brand."

I stepped closer to the board. The differences were striking. Variations in shade. In typography. In symbols. In some markets, even the lion itself had been locally reinterpreted.

"There's a lot of emotional attachment to these," Nanne said. "People feel they belong to their market's version."

"I understand that," I replied. "But this is one of the most frequent moments we have with customers. They may not think about their bank every day, but they take out their card all the time. This is where identity lives."

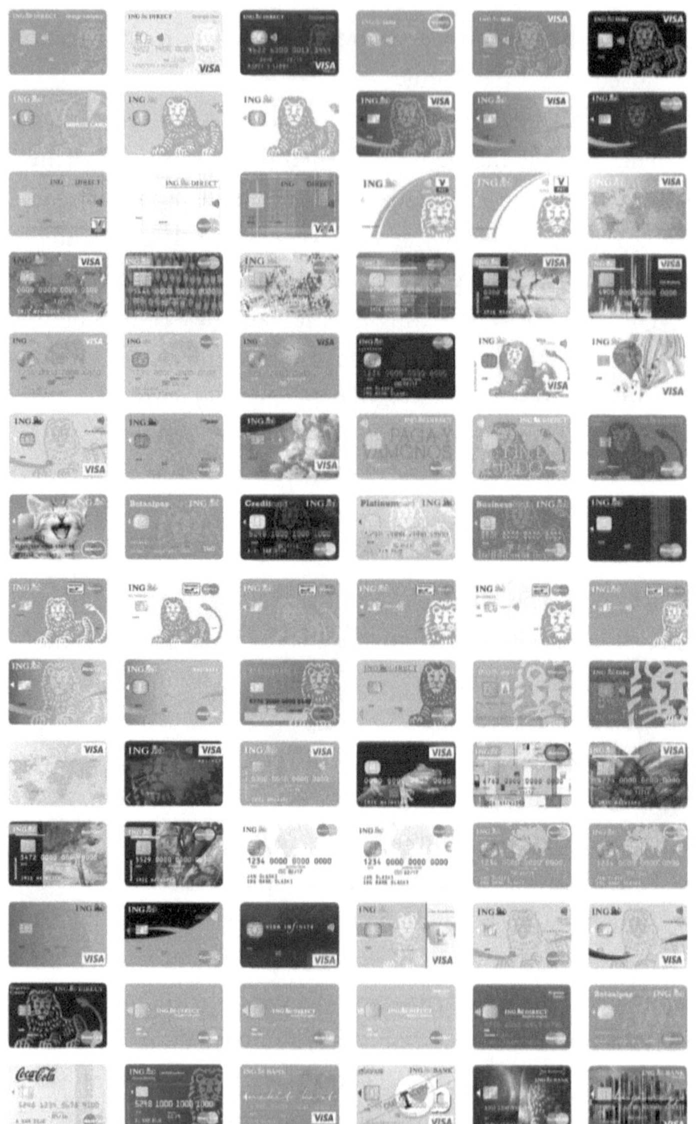

Nanne agreed. "Payment is brand."

If we wanted people to associate their banking experience with ING, this had to change. A customer in Australia is not fundamentally different from a customer in Luxembourg, Italy, or Turkey. What we need is recognition, not variation.

"We need to move toward one system," I said. "One visual language. A consistent look and feel, across markets."

"Predominantly orange," Nanne added, "one logo."

"Exactly," I said. "Pay with orange. Bank with orange."

That conversation crystallized what had already become clear. This was not about design control or aesthetics. It was about coherence, trust, and being recognizably ING wherever and however customers interacted with us.

Over time, we rebuilt the payment cards as part of a broader effort to align the brand, visually and emotionally, with who we were becoming: a more unified, empowering, digitally native bank with a clear and consistent promise.

After working extensively with leaders in different markets to ensure everyone everywhere felt seen, we ended with a family of seven cards.

They were all deliberately simple and unmistakably ING. Even from the side, the cards were recognizably orange. You could spot them immediately in a stack of credit-card-sized cards without having to turn them over.

We also added a small notch on the side, making it easier to distinguish for people who are visually impaired.

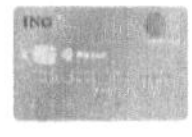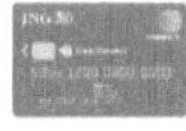

WHY THE BRAND BELONGS TO THE CEO

If aligning our brand with our purpose and strategy was as easy as streamlining our bank cards, we would have been successful within two years.

It took us seven.

It was a massive undertaking that required scrutiny across all areas of ING...as the CEO, it also required my direct attention.

I have always believed that a CEO cannot delegate three things:

1. Strategy
2. Talent and Culture/Behavior
3. Brand/Reputation and Communication

Strategy defines where you are going. Talent and culture determine whether you can get there. Brand is the most visible expression of both. It is how the outside world experiences your decisions, your priorities, and your consistency over time. That is why brand does not belong to marketing. It belongs to the CEO.

Brand is often misunderstood as a communications exercise: a logo, a campaign, a tagline. That is a mistake. A brand is not what you say about yourself; it is what people experience when they interact with you: customers, employees, regulators, partners, and society at large. Over time, those experiences accumulate into a reputation. That reputation, whether you like it or not, becomes your brand.

When I became CEO of ING in 2013, this distinction mattered deeply. The organization had gone through years of expansion, crisis, restructuring, and divestment. We had become a pure bank again, but the brand did not reflect that reality. Externally, we still looked like a fragmented financial conglomerate. Internally, different parts of the organization carried different identities, different assumptions, and different interpretations of what "ING" stood for. The brand was no longer a unifying force; it was a shared logo applied to very different experiences.

That misalignment is not something marketing can fix.

Only the CEO can ensure that the brand is anchored in the organization's strategy and lived through behavior, investment choices, and trade-offs. Marketing can help articulate the promise, communications can help amplify it, but only the CEO can make sure that the promise is kept. Every leadership decision strengthens or weakens the brand. Where you invest. What you simplify. What you tolerate. What you stop. What you reward. What you ignore. These choices send far stronger signals than any campaign ever could. If the CEO does not own those signals, then no one truly owns the brand.

For me, brand was never something to be layered on top of the organization. Going back to my framework, it became clear to me that a brand must be derived from purpose and built through consistent alignment: between strategy, prioritization, and execution. When those elements reinforce one another, the brand becomes authentic and credible. And when they do not, the misalignment is immediately visible. The brand was a mirror. It showed us where our strategy was clear and where it was not. It revealed whether our culture supported our ambitions or quietly resisted them. It also exposed the gap between what we aspired to be and what people experienced when they used our products, worked with us, or encountered us in society.

As ING moved toward becoming a digital bank, that mirror became impossible to ignore. In a digital world, customers do not experience you occasionally; they experience you constantly. They see you on their phone screens or watches, sometimes dozens of times a day. In that context, inconsistency is immediately visible. You cannot behave like a loose federation of banks or products and still claim to be one brand. You either show up as one organization, or you are fragmented in full view of your customers.

This is why brand is part of the framework and why brand was a strategic initiative at ING, not a marketing one. It was inseparable from our transformation. Owning the brand meant taking responsibility for alignment: between purpose and behavior, between strategy and experience, and between what we said and what we did.

CAN A BANK BECOME A LOVE BRAND?

In our strategy discussions, we introduced an ambition that raised eyebrows: ING should aspire to become a love brand. At the time, that statement was meant to be directional, not rhetorical. It was a way of challenging ourselves to think differently about the role a bank could play in people's lives.

Once we moved from aspiration to execution, however, a more uncomfortable question followed: was this ambition realistic?

The skepticism was understandable. Banking is not an industry people love. In reputation rankings, banks often sit close to industries like tobacco or arms—necessary, perhaps, but rarely admired and certainly hardly embraced. For decades, banks had been seen as complex, distant, and self-serving. Many people interact with their bank only when something goes wrong, so the idea of becoming a love brand sounded naïve at best.

The question was fair: can a bank really become a love brand?

My answer was not emotional. It was pragmatic.

In a digital world, indifference is dangerous. If customers do not trust you, do not like you, and do not feel you are on their side, you have a structural problem. Switching costs are low, alternatives are one click away, and negative experiences travel fast. You do not need people to adore you, but if they feel nothing at all, you are replaceable.

We also had evidence that something different was possible. ING Direct had shown it. By being simple, transparent, and relentlessly customer-centric, it had built loyalty and even affection in markets where banking was deeply distrusted. Customers spoke positively about ING. That alone was extraordinary.

More than that, people began to identify themselves with ING as a challenger. A different kind of bank. A place where you were encouraged to perform, to grow, and to pursue your ambitions. It suggested that while people may not love banks as institutions, they can value and even advocate for banks that consistently respect their time, intelligence, and autonomy.

That distinction mattered. Love was never the objective. A connection through trust, ease, and empowerment were. If we could make banking frictionless, treat people as equals, and help them move forward in their lives and businesses, then positive emotion would follow. Because we earned it.

In that sense, becoming a love brand was not about sentiment. It was about discipline and consistency. Love, in this sense, is not something you declare; it is a consequence of doing the right things, in the right way, over time. The real question was whether we were willing to make the long-term choices required to deserve it and stay the course. If we were successful, we should not just be number one in NPS but lead with a ten-point difference.

"ING was very much a federation of local businesses rather than a united idea. They shared the same logo and colors, but they stood for different things in different markets."

—RUSS PINNEY, MANAGING DIRECTOR, TWOFISH
CREATIVE ADVERTISING AGENCY

When I became CEO, the ambition was clear. The reality was fragmented, because during the restructuring there hadn't been one clear overarching banking story.

I could feel it almost immediately. Not in one dramatic moment but in dozens of small ones. Conversations that sounded aligned on the surface but diverged underneath. Presentations that used the same words yet meant different things. Decisions that stalled because no one was quite sure which "ING" they were speaking for.

Remember the eighty-four different bank cards? That was the tip of the iceberg.

At first, it sounded almost amusing: eighty-four cards. Creative. Entrepreneurial. The longer we looked at it, however, the less amusing it became. If we couldn't agree on something as basic as a card, what did that say about the experience customers were having?

ING is orange, but there were many different oranges. Different shades. Different interpretations. Different meanings. We used multiple font types. We had more than seven slogans across markets. Visual identities varied widely. Tone of voice differed from country to country.

Even basic elements like brochures and interfaces looked

unrelated. Put next to each other, it was jarring. Pamphlets and screens that didn't speak the same visual language. Materials that could have belonged to entirely different companies. If you stripped away the logo, you would never guess they were part of the same bank.

Every local organization believed it was unique. Every head of marketing believed they were serving a distinct audience with a distinct proposition. In isolation, each story made sense. Collectively, they did not.

I understood where it came from. Many of these teams had built real success. They had earned their autonomy. Asking them to align did not feel, to them, like progress. It felt like loss.

What we had was not a brand. We had a collection of brands sharing a logo.

This fragmentation had historical reasons. ING had grown through acquisitions, greenfield launches, and local successes. Country managers had effectively built their own banks, insurance companies, and asset managers. In a world of physical distribution, like agents, branches, paper statements, and local advertising, that model worked well enough. Customers experienced us locally, and the seams between markets were mostly invisible.

That world was disappearing, however. Customers no longer experienced ING country by country. They experienced us through screens, where inconsistency is immediately visible. A customer might move from one market to another, from retail to wholesale, or from web to mobile, and suddenly the differences were no longer abstract. They were confusing and eroded trust.

Imagine being that customer. Logging in from one country, then another. Switching from desktop to mobile. Each step requiring a small mental reset. None of it catastrophic. All of it cumulative. Trust rarely disappears in one moment; it fades through friction.

This was not a branding issue. It was a strategic one.

Fragmentation creates inefficiency. It slows decision-making, multiplies cost, and makes scale harder than it needs to be. More importantly, it weakens confidence, inside and outside the organization. When people inside the bank cannot clearly articulate who they are and what they stand for, customers feel it instantly.

Internally, when I started, the lack of a shared identity made alignment difficult. Teams worked hard but often in different directions, and wholesale banking carried a different culture altogether. Local retail banks often tried to be everything to everyone (neutral, careful, and inoffensive), which made them blend into the background rather than stand out.

It was frustrating because energy was everywhere, but alignment was not. Without alignment, even the best intentions cancel each other out.

Externally, the brand no longer reflected who we were. ING had become a focused bank again, but the brand still looked like a financial conglomerate that no longer existed. It was like someone who had lost fifty pounds but was still wearing the same oversized clothes: nothing fit anymore.

The brand hadn't caught up, and everyone could feel the discomfort.

This mismatch mattered. Brand is the external expression of identity. When identity and reality drift apart, credibility suffers. Credibility is not something you can fix with messaging; it requires alignment between strategy, structure, behavior, and user experience. This is the reason why brand and reputation are part of my framework; as CEO, those responsibilities sat with me. If people could not clearly say who we were and what we were here for, that wasn't a communications failure. It was a leadership one.

What struck me most was that none of the fragmentation came from bad intent. People throughout the organization cared deeply about "their" ING. The resistance to change was often strongest where identity was strongest. That, paradoxically, was a good sign. If we wanted to become one bank, with the same customer promise and strategic priorities and operating as one platform as much as possible, we could not continue as a loose federation of local interpretations. We needed to move from many ING stories to one ING narrative, not by erasing local strengths but by anchoring them in a shared identity and direction. What stayed with me most was that no one was acting in bad faith. People cared. Deeply. That meant our brand transformation would require patience, listening, and a willingness to disappoint in the short term to build something stronger in the long term.

That realization became the starting point for everything that followed...and from the beginning (in 2013), I knew this would be a long journey.

It was. ING's brand transformation, like the overall transformation, was a marathon, not a sprint.

CHOOSING AN ORGANIZATIONAL BRAND: A LONG-TERM COMMITMENT

Brand transformation follows the same rules as business transformation. Consistency over time matters more than intensity. It is not about one bold move but about thousands of small, aligned decisions, made day after day, until a new pattern becomes visible and credible.

During our strategy meetings, we made a deliberate choice

to treat ING as an organizational brand. One brand. One promise. Many expressions.

That choice was fundamental. It meant that ING would no longer behave as a collection of loosely connected local brands but as one organization speaking with a shared voice across countries, businesses, and channels. Not uniform in every detail but coherent in what we stood for and how we showed up.

This was not about central control. It was about clarity.

An organizational brand supports strategy. It creates trust across markets. It allows customers, investors, and employees to recognize the organization instantly, regardless of where or how they interact with it. In a digital world, that consistency becomes even more important, because people experience you continuously.

An organizational brand also demands discipline, however.

You cannot impose it overnight, mandate belief, or treat it as a rebranding exercise (new logos, new colors, and a launch campaign) while everything underneath stays the same. An organizational brand only works if it is backed by real alignment: in priorities, behaviors, investments, and trade-offs.

That meant accepting that progress would sometimes feel slow. It meant resisting the temptation to declare success too early. It also meant being prepared to stay the course, even when the results were not yet visible.

Choosing an organizational brand was not a communications decision. It was a leadership commitment to coherence, patience, and building something that would last.

HOW WE WERE PERCEIVED

The first step was that we needed to be honest about where we were. Not through internal debates or leadership offsites but through the eyes of the people who experienced ING from the outside.

How were we perceived across markets? By customers and noncustomers. By partners, regulators, and society more broadly.

At that point, everyone had an opinion. Local teams were convinced they understood their markets best. Leaders believed they knew what differentiated their businesses. But opinions or assumptions are not facts.

If we were serious about building one brand, we needed a shared, fact-based understanding of how ING showed up in the real world. Not how we intended to show up. Not how we described ourselves internally. But how we were experienced and perceived.

That required research at scale. Comparable across markets. Designed to reveal patterns rather than anecdotes and rigorous enough to challenge deeply held beliefs.

This was not a comfortable exercise. It rarely is. When you ask people outside the organization how they perceive you, the answers do not always match the stories you tell yourself. Discomfort is often a signal that you are finally looking at the right data.

UNDERSTANDING PEOPLE AND THEIR ROUTINES

Once we started to operate as a true digital platform, the nature of our relationship with our customers changed. In a single year, we saw more than six billion interactions with our customers, of which 98 percent were digital and the majority already on mobile. These customers were accessing our app several times a day. We had to think of them differently; we needed to understand them, and it was critical that the brand reflect that.

We needed a different lens. Instead of asking, "What is this customer worth to us?" we had to ask, "How does this person use us in their daily life, and where do we create friction?"

In the analogue world, people tolerated complexity: paper forms, branch visits, opening hours. In the digital world, they compare us to the best apps they use, not to other banks. That reshaped expectations completely.

If a music or travel app can be intuitive, real-time, and personalized, why shouldn't their bank be the same? Every delay, every extra click, every unclear message is no longer just an inconvenience; it's a signal that we don't understand their reality. That is why we deliberately shifted our language, and our thinking, from customers to users. It forced us to design around customer behavior, not around menus and products.

We commissioned large-scale NeedScope research to understand the conscious and unconscious associations people had with ING across markets. It helped us move beyond demographics and product categories and gave us a clear language for emotion: control versus freedom, individual versus group.

> "What surprised us most was the consistency: despite our decentralized past, people associated ING with freedom, independence, and room to move. Once we saw that signal so clearly, the question became obvious: if that's what people already feel, why wouldn't we build on it with discipline?"
>
> —NANNE BOS, FORMER ING HEAD OF BRAND

We then started working with Russ Pinney at Twofish, an advertising and creative firm based in the Netherlands. We had plenty of rich, detailed data, and now we needed help analyzing it. His role was to help us turn insight into understanding and understanding into alignment, so we were first speaking consistently to ourselves before the outside world.

CLARIFYING WHO WE WERE FOR

The next step was focus. We could not be everything to everyone.

For years, like most banks, we had organized ourselves around products, segments, and internal categories. Retail versus wholesale. Mass market versus affluent. Accounts, loans, mortgages, savings. That logic works for managing balance sheets. It does not work for building a meaningful brand.

So we deliberately shifted the question. Not what products do we sell to which segments, but what role do we play in people's lives or company's journeys?

When do they turn to us?

What are they trying to achieve at that moment?

Where do we create friction, and where do we genuinely help them move forward and let them do what they need to do?

That change in perspective forced us to look at behavior rather than labels. At needs rather than demographics. At moments rather than transactions. It also made something very clear: not every customer need matters equally for our strategy, and not every audience can sit at the center of the brand.

This is where strategy becomes uncomfortable and real. Focus demands choice.

Choice demands trade-offs, like I described in Chapter 5: Customer at the Core.

Saying yes to one role means saying no to others. Designing for certain needs means accepting that some customers will recognize themselves more strongly in the brand than others. That is not exclusion; it is clarity.

Without that clarity, brand becomes generic, diluted, and

forgettable. With it, every decision, product design, tone of voice, experience, investment, has a reference point. You know who you are trying to help and why.

It sharpened our ambition.

CONNECTING TO THE FREEDOM MINDSET

We complemented NeedScope research we did on brand perception with research from localities, which gave us a deeper understanding of people's values and life priorities.

Taken together, these studies gave us a simple, powerful design brief:

- People associate ING with freedom and independence.
- They want more time to do the things that move them and with less friction. This is for retail and corporate customers alike.
- They expect digital experiences that respect their autonomy.

Our brand strategy had to sit exactly at that intersection. And it was almost a literal translation of what our purpose should deliver.

The next question was *who are we really here for?* At the time in 2016, ING served more than 35 million customers in about eight demographic segments, and all of them were important. But if you try to build a brand for everyone, you end up resonating with no one. So we made a deliberate choice to define a strategic target based not on demographics but on psychographics. We called this aspirational target audience "Freedom People."

This was not a traditional marketing exercise. We were not trying to exclude customers or narrow our commercial focus to a single segment. Rather, we needed a clear point of view about the kind of people we wanted to design for and stand behind based on how ING was already perceived.

The logical next question, then, was what kind of people are drawn to a bank that represents freedom? What mindset do they share across age, income, and geography? Defining Freedom People helped us answer that question in a way the entire organization could understand and act on.

Freedom People believe they can shape their own future and run their own businesses. They are independent, curious, open-minded, and positive about innovation and technology. They want to take responsibility in life, career, and business, and they expect the institutions around them to help rather than hinder that progress. They want to be empowered.

At the same time, they feel the strain of modern life and work: too many rules, too much bureaucracy, and too little time. They move quickly between work and personal life, they live on their phones and work behind a desktop, and they want information that is clear, direct, and easy to act on.

Exactly our customer promise.

Choosing Freedom People as our strategic target audience did two things for us.

First, it further sharpened the promise: if we are here for people who want to drive progress, then our role is to remove friction and empower them, not to push products or prescribe choices.

Second, it created coherence. From product design and risk policies to tone of voice and sponsorships, we could ask a simple question: Does this help our customers do more of what moves them? Does it help them to grow their business? If not, we had to rethink it.

This focus did not exclude anyone. Instead, it gave us a clear center of gravity. By building a brand for Freedom People, we made ING more relevant, human, and consistent for everyone who recognized themselves in that desire to move forward.

DEFINING OUR ROLE: FROM BANK TO ENABLER

Out of this work came a clear role for ING as a brand. We are not the heroes of our customers' stories. They are.

This represents a very specific brand choice. Some brands position themselves as protagonists: aspirational, visible, and expressive. Enabler brands take a different role. They exist to help people do what they already want to do better and with less effort. When they work well, they fade into the background of the story, even though they made the story possible in the first place.

Whether consumer or corporate, ING's role is to enable them to remove friction and make progress easier. When banking works well, it becomes almost invisible, but it is indispensable.

It confirmed our thesis about the role banks had when we started our strategy exercise. And this was being confirmed by the customers we were building our brand for. Success was no longer about visibility for its own sake or about inserting ourselves into every interaction. It was about reliability, simplicity, and trust: being present when needed and staying out of the way when not.

This role brought clarity. It connected purpose, strategy, and brand into one coherent idea, and it gave us a consistent lens through which to evaluate everything that followed.

One specific design question became surprisingly important: what should be the primary digital identifier of ING?

Our research and our own data told us that people do not need "a bank"; they need banking. Increasingly, that banking happens through our app.

We did a dedicated study of the traditional ING lion logo in digital contexts. We explored different crops of the lion, full body, different head crops, and tested how they performed as a small, digital icon across an app ecosystem.

The conclusion was clear: a specific head crop of the lion worked best as our digital identifier, balancing recognizability with simplicity at very small sizes.

That decision might sound technical, but it was symbolic. By treating that icon as a central brand asset, like the Nike Swoosh, and not an afterthought, we aligned our visual system with the reality of a mobile-first, platform-driven bank. We decided on a specific crop of the head of the lion with ING orange as the background. No letters, just the image.

PLAYING WITH LEGOS

As our brand ambition became clearer, we faced a practical challenge that every global organization eventually encounters: how do you create coherence at scale without stripping people of ownership?

This was not an abstract question. It went to the heart of how change actually happens in large organizations. You can dictate everything from the center, but then people disengage. Or you can allow total freedom, but then coherence disappears. Neither extreme works if you want transformation to stick.

The answer came through what was called the LEGO system.

The spirit of this decision mattered as much as the mechanics. We needed a system that was strict enough to create a strong, recognizable brand yet flexible enough that people could still see themselves in it. If teams felt the brand was being imposed on them, we would lose energy. If they felt they were co-creating it, we could take people with us.

The idea was simple. LEGO bricks are the same everywhere. The components are fixed; they cannot be altered. But what you build with them can vary endlessly. From a distance, every creation is unmistakably LEGO. Up close, each one reflects local creativity and context.

We applied that principle to the ING brand.

At the core of the system were a small number of nonnegotiable building blocks: a single logo, one visual identity, consistent typography, a defined color palette, and later, a shared photographic language and global tagline. These elements were standardized globally for both retail and wholesale banking. They could not be modified or reinterpreted.

This level of discipline was essential. Strong brands are not flexible at their core; they are incredibly strict. Ambiguity at the center leads to fragmentation at the edges. By being uncompromising about a small number of elements, we earned the right to be generous everywhere else.

Around those fixed components, we deliberately created space. Local teams could choose how to assemble the blocks, how to tell their stories, and how to activate the brand in ways that made sense for their markets. The goal was not sameness. It was recognizability.

That balance captured something deeper about how we approached transformation more broadly. We believed innovation does not come from total freedom but from clear constraints. By fixing the essentials, we freed teams to innovate where it mattered most: in services and customer experience. This was necessary because the different local banks operated with different distribution models and were at very different stages in the digitalization of their services.

From the beginning, we were pragmatic about what the organization could absorb. Getting to this system was not easy. It required letting go of local preferences that people cared deeply about and asking for trust before results were visible.

We did not attempt to harmonize everything at once. Early on, we focused on the basics: cleaning up the logo, reducing variations, aligning fundamental design rules. More expressive elements, such as photography and a single tagline, came later as the broader transformation gained momentum, confidence increased, and a cross-border standardization of customer experience (app, customer promise) increased.

FONT

When we first started discussing the font, it did not begin as a design conversation. It began with a much more fundamental question: *what would be the most important carrier of the ING brand going forward?*

That raised a new challenge: how do you own your brand expression in a space as constrained as a watch?

There was no consistent font across the organization, so it would be a massive, painstaking undertaking...yet we started working on it. Nanne and I met with international marketing teams *extensively* and selected a font that was developed for people with reading disabilities. We thought, "We want to empower everyone. We want to make it accessible to all." That was the connection.

From there, we developed the numbers, so we had a complete typeface. Because we send so many documents to customers and display information on devices where people must look at numbers, it needed to be very accessible. We called our new typeface "ING Me." We developed it, owned the rights to it. It's a real differentiator.

COLOR

Orange had always been our primary brand color. It was distinctive, deeply associated with ING, and immediately recognizable across markets.

At the same time, we became very clear about what we did not want: a brand that overwhelmed people by turning everything orange. If orange was to remain powerful, it had to be used with discipline.

The discussion about color evolved in parallel with the broader brand system. As we moved toward screens and daily digital interactions, color had to work harder to support clarity, accessibility, and emotional balance across very different use cases.

The Spanish team challenged the idea that consistency meant visual monotony. They showed that you could preserve strong brand recognition while allowing more variation and warmth in the palette. That insight led us to extend the secondary color palette to a broader range of colors while keeping orange firmly at the center.

This was fully aligned with the LEGO system. Orange remained a nonnegotiable building block. The extended secondary palette provided flexibility. Local teams could express tone, context, and emotion without breaking coherence. From a distance, it was unmistakably ING. Up close, it felt more human and adaptable.

In banking, there's a tendency for the tone of voice to be quite formal. When banks try to sound formal or more important, it creates distance. ING has always gone against that current. In Germany, we intentionally used the informal Du instead of Sie, which changes the tone compared to other German banks.

Our tone had to be peer-to-peer: informal, not prescriptive, and focused on enabling rather than instructing. By using active language, we showed that we were the bank that enables, supports, and puts the customer always in charge.

SONIC LOGO

One of ING's longest-standing traditions is beginning the year with a New Year's Concert performed by the Royal Concertgebouw Orchestra in the concert hall in Amsterdam.

The evening traditionally begins with a welcome speech from the CEO wishing everyone a Happy New Year, followed by a beautiful concert and a series of smaller performances and receptions (different musical styles played across the Royal Concertgebouw's halls and rooms).

It was Saturday evening, January 11, 2020, when I had the honor of welcoming approximately 2,000 colleagues to ING's New Year's Concert.

At the end of my speech, I had a surprise prepared: something related to our brand. It was not something the audience could see; they could only hear it. As I stood on stage, one of the finest orchestras in the world began to play ING's sonic logo.

The final step in our brand evolution was recognizing that since we didn't have a physical presence in many markets, we needed to build brand recognition through sound as well. That led us to create a sonic logo: a distinctive sound that played at the end of our commercials or possibly when opening the app, something people instantly recognized as ING.

We moved away from traditional banking imagery and began presenting ourselves like an app, since that's how we live in people's mobile phones.

RE-ANCHORING THE ORANGE CODE

By the time we reached this phase of our transformation in 2019, the Orange Code (Chapter 4) was already part of everyday language at ING. People knew the words, values, and behaviors. What mattered now was reconnecting them to why they existed in the first place: the brand.

Our work on love brands had made something very clear. There was a strong correlation between how much a brand was valued externally and the extent to which employees were aligned with (and actively living) the brand promise *internally*. Love on the outside could not be sustained without belief and behavior on the inside. External affinity follows internal conviction, not the other way around. Brands with strong emotional connection on the outside consistently show high internal engagement and advocacy. Without that internal foundation, without people who feel ownership, pride, and belief, any brand promise remains hollow.

As I explained in the framework, that insight reinforced why the Orange Code mattered. It was not just a set of behaviors; it was the mechanism through which we executed strategy, delivered on our customer promise, and thus translated our brand promise into daily action. If ING's brand was going to be built around freedom, empowerment, and enabling others to move forward, then those ideas had to be lived every day inside the organization.

The Orange Code became essential precisely for that reason. But it was not a branding exercise; it was a cultural one. We needed a small number of clear principles that described how we expected people at ING to think and act, regardless of role, geography, or function. Principles that could guide decisions when no one was watching. Principles that reinforced that progress requires ownership, collaboration, and anticipation.

These statements described the behavior behind the brand. Taking responsibility and turning intent into action. Helping others succeed rather than optimizing for individual silos. Staying ahead by looking forward, learning continuously, and acting before being forced to.

This was how we would build the brand, through culture first, and only then through communication.

Taken together, they describe how a digital, empowering bank behaves from the inside out. Ownership over hierarchy. Collaboration over silos. Anticipation over reaction.

> "Culture starts at the top. It's not a branding exercise: all that branding can do is reflect what the person at the top believes. If the person at the top doesn't believe in it, then it's just window dressing."
>
> —RUSS PINNEY, MANAGING DIRECTOR, TWOFISH CREATIVE ADVERTISING AGENCY

DO YOUR THING

Starting from our purpose, with a clear customer promise and supporting internal behaviors, the brand positioning was clear. What remained was to find a simple expression that could carry everything we had built, externally and internally, without diluting it.

That was harder than it sounds.

We were not looking for a marketing line. We were looking for a rallying cry that would encourage people without prescribing their choices. Something that respected the fact that our customers, whether individuals or businesses, already have ambitions, opinions, and plans. They don't need a bank to tell them what to do. What they need is support, clarity, and the removal of obstacles.

In the end, all the work we had done on purpose, culture, the Orange Code, the comprehensive transformation, and becoming invisible yet indispensable boiled down to three words:

"Do Your Thing."

Those words were not a starting point. They were a distillation. Everything had to be true before we could say them out loud. Until we were absolutely certain we could live up to the customer promise, those words could not exist. "Do Your Thing" could not be lipstick on a gorilla. It had to reflect reality, not aspiration.

What mattered most was that the expression put the spotlight where it belonged: on our customers, not on us. It acknowledges that progress comes from people who take responsibility for shaping their own future and the world around them, whether through small daily decisions or bold entrepreneurial moves. Our role is simply to make banking easy enough that it doesn't get in the way of that progress.

Research showed that our tagline resonated well across our markets. ING customers see themselves as responsible for their own fate and that of their surroundings. Our promise acknowledges that and says, "We will make banking easy so that you can focus on what really matters to you."

That became clear that freezing-cold January morning when we opened our campus.

When the words Do Your Thing appeared, quietly, without fanfare, it didn't feel like a launch. It felt like recognition. A moment when purpose, culture, customer promise, and brand finally aligned.

Do Your Thing is not the brand itself. It is the visible tip of an iceberg built through Think Forward. It is how our purpose sounds when it speaks directly to the people and businesses we serve. Nothing more, nothing less.

INTRODUCING "DO YOUR THING"

Do Your Thing did not start as a line in a brief. It was the final expression of a seven-year transformation, from 2013 to 2020, where we aligned insight, identity, behavior, and experience across the entire organization. Over those years we clarified our purpose, defined a clear brand belief and role, focused our strategy on empowering people who want to drive progress, reshaped our culture through the Orange Code, built a unified visual identity for a digital-first bank, and proved through early activations and customer research that empowerment could be felt and measured in the market. Only once those pieces were working together did we feel ready to articulate a simple promise that captured all of it.

We were already growing fast in numbers of customers for many years, but this needed to continue.

All this mattered for the timing.

I did not want to reveal a new slogan while we were still internally fragmented or externally inconsistent: we chose the inauguration of the new ING campus as the moment to introduce "Do Your Thing"

On the day of the inauguration, I stood on the platform of the central staircase overlooking the internal street, surrounded by colleagues along the railings. That vantage point mattered to me. This was not a stage in front of a distant audience; it was a space where people could see each other, connect with each other, and move freely through the building.

When we introduced Do Your Thing, we explained it not as a clever campaign but as the expression of everything we had been working toward:

- Our purpose to empower people to stay a step ahead in life and in business
- Our role to make banking frictionless and seamless, operating in the background, enabling you to do more of what you love to do
- Our belief that progress is always possible, however modest or ambitious the step

For me, speaking those words from the stairs in that building was the moment when the physical, cultural, and strategic dimensions of the brand clicked into place.

"When the line worked, it wasn't because it was clever; it worked because it was true to the role we had defined: enabler, not hero."

—NANNE BOS, FORMER ING HEAD OF BRAND

Working on the brand taught me patience in a way few other parts of the transformation did. It moves slowly. Often quietly. And long before results show up in market share or reputation rankings, it shows up somewhere else first: in decisions.

Brand exposes misalignment faster than any dashboard. If your strategy says one thing but your incentives reward another, the brand will feel hollow. If leaders talk about empowerment but operate through control, people notice. If you claim to stand for something but make trade-offs that contradict it, the inconsistency becomes visible internally before it ever reaches customers.

This is why brand cannot be treated as a communications exercise. It sits at the intersection of strategy, culture, and leadership behavior, as depicted in the framework. Owning it means being willing to make hard choices and repeat them, even when they are inconvenient. Consistency protects coherence over time, not chasing short-term visibility.

When done well, brand becomes an alignment mechanism. It gives people a shared reference point for decisions: what to prioritize, how to act, and where to draw boundaries. It helps thousands of individuals, across markets and functions, understand how their daily choices connect to something bigger than their role or their team.

A love brand is not primarily about how the world sees you;

it's about how your customers see themselves. It is also about how clearly you see yourself and whether you are willing to lead in a way that makes that clarity real, day after day.

The true test of alignment, however, does not happen in advertising or even in customer experience. It happens when your purpose collides with capital and the decisions you make shape entire industries.

When brand becomes impact at scale.

IMPACT AT SCALE

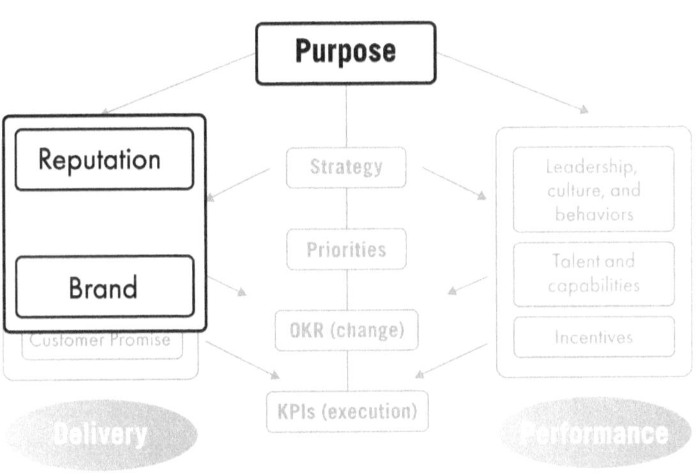

Banks have a broader role to play in society. We started with our purpose that helped us generating positive impact using our strengths and unique qualities.

It was December 4, 2018. The skies were gray, and all the leaves had fallen in Katowice, the province of Silesia, Poland. I was on my way to announce ING's commitment to manage the future size and composition of our loan portfolio in line with the Paris Climate Accord, signed in 2015.

Katowice is where ING Poland is historically rooted, through ING Bank Śląski. Our Polish headquarters is there, and the city is an important part of ING's history. It's also the center of Poland's coal mining industry. In 2018, 78 percent of the country's electricity came from coal-fired power plants. That year, the United Nations chose Katowice as the location for COP24, the annual conference where global leaders gather to agree on actions to limit global warming and address climate change.

At the time, we didn't know our announcement would have such an impact. ING became the first bank in the world to commit to reducing its Scope 3 carbon footprint in a measurable, science-based way.

That first step, later known as the Terra Approach, was quickly followed by others. ING's commitment, initially joined by four other banks, became the foundation of the Collective Commitment to Climate Action (UNEP FI, 2019), which was later integrated into the Net-Zero Banking Alliance launched in August 2021.

If you recall, ING's purpose began with the customer, not as a slogan but as a foundation for everything we did. We asked, *How can we play a meaningful role in people's lives or business and help them make progress?* That clarity became the starting point for a broader ambition: to build a bank that wasn't just financially sound but socially relevant.

Many banks responded to the financial crisis by shifting their focus to society first. But without a deep understanding of customer needs, that focus often remained abstract. At ING, we flipped the script. We started with real customer insights, needs, frictions, aspirations, and built from there. That led to innovations in mobile banking like frictionless design and open banking platforms, all grounded in day-to-day relevance.

Before those innovations, however, we asked these questions: What makes ING different in the industry? And what is our broader impact on society?

By layering customer relevance, strategic differentiation, and societal contribution, we defined a purpose that was bold, actionable, and transformative. Not just words on a wall but a business strategy that helped reshape what a modern, responsible bank could be.

FROM PURPOSE TO IMPACT

"It comes back to purpose, right? It's what gets you out of bed in the morning. Do you feel like the work you're doing matters, to society, to your team, to your business unit, or whatever part of the organization you identify with? Is it relevant? And does it align with your personal values or your desire to grow? If the answer to those questions is no, that's usually why people leave."

—DOROTHY HILL, FORMER ING HEAD OF STRATEGY

When we talk about "purpose to impact," I often associate it with the sustainability side of our work. In truth, the concept operates on multiple levels across an organization, and it was foundational to everything we built.

At one level, it's about external relevance: how your purpose translates into broader societal initiatives like financial literacy, financial independence, or environmental sustainability. These expressions of purpose are how a company earns trust, not just market share; they support the brand and reputation, hence their importance to the framework.

There's another often overlooked layer: the unintended consequences of progress. Digitalization, for example, improves access and convenience, but it also erodes financial literacy. When money becomes abstracted from the physical world, it's easier to lose track of its true value. You don't count twelve one-dollar bills anymore; you see "$12" in an app. Spend $6.50 on a coffee, and it feels like simple math (12 – 6.5). It's much harder to understand the association between hard work and a number on an app versus physical cash.

That disconnect has profound societal consequences, especially for younger generations who've never handled cash. How do we make sure the concept of value, the discipline of saving, and the awareness of effort survive in a digital world where money is no longer physical? How do we own the flip side of our success?

This was the thinking behind the Think Forward Initiative. The Think Forward Initiative was a multidisciplinary and open movement that promoted research and practical solutions to empower people to make better financial decisions. We launched the Think Forward Initiative on November 19, 2015, starting it together with partners Microsoft, EMC, the Institute for New Economic Thinking, and INOMICS.

The official kickoff summit took place on February 25, 2016, in Brussels, bringing together more than 120 academics, European and national policymakers, consumer-organization representatives, and leaders from the financial and technology sectors. All to create practical solutions for better financial decision-making.

Given the open-source character, other sponsors quickly followed: Deloitte, Dell, Dimension Data, Amazon Web Services (AWS), and the Center for Economic Policy Research (CEPR).

We were aligned in recognizing that digital money, just a number on a screen, can weaken people's connection to financial effort and discipline. Together, we explored ways to reintroduce that connection, reinforcing responsible behavior through design, nudges, and education. Academic research helped to find the right way to raise awareness, educate, and guide people through for example functions in banking and consumer agency apps.

That's where purpose becomes powerful: when it drives innovation, aligns partners, and creates value not only for customers but for society.

At its peak, the Think Forward Initiative was supported by a network of nearly 1,500 contributors, including researchers, policymakers, entrepreneurs, consumer advocates, NGOs, innovators, corporations, and influencers.

The Think Forward Initiative achieved its key milestones and supported almost sixty research projects while reaching more than 100 million people worldwide. Although this initiative was discontinued in December 2021, consumer self-reliance, financial literacy, and financial empowerment stayed core components of ING's current sustainability strategy.

> *"If we wanted to live up to our purpose, we needed to showcase we were serious about it and lead the conversation. That's why we launched the Think Forward Initiative: it was all about helping people become more self-reliant and equipping them to make sound financial decisions."*
>
> —PETER JONG, FORMER ING HEAD OF COMMUNICATION

ONE STEP FURTHER

Internally, "purpose to impact" also meant translating high-level aspiration into concrete execution. That's what our Strategy on a Page was all about. Purpose didn't just live on posters; it guided our operational plans, KPIs, and cultural behaviors. It helped ensure we built an organization that could deliver on what we said we stood for.

Whether viewed as a social ambition or a strategic engine, purpose must be more than a slogan. It must be proactive, measurable, and visible, both inside and outside the company. If it is authentic, it generates real momentum, the kind that sustains transformation and drives lasting impact.

"Purpose to Impact" really meant driving growth and accepting responsibility for the broader effects of our work.

THE WEIGHT OF LEAVING THE WORLD BETTER

Part of our motivation came from a deep awareness of the industry's failure during the financial crisis.

In the aftermath, ING, like many banks, was seen as part of a broken system. The public believed we had let them down. Trust in financial institutions had eroded. Banks were perceived as selfish actors, focused only on profits, blind to their broader societal impact. To a large extent, that perception wasn't wrong. That kind of unchecked behavior is what led the industry, and the global economy, into crisis.

"When we started talking about purpose and societal impact, it wasn't a trendy PR play. It was a necessary course correction. We had to prove we could scale as a business and still leave the world better than we found it. To do so, we had to show that long-term growth and long-term impact were not in conflict but could go hand in hand.

"The next question became: how do we do this responsibly?

"That's where Terra came in. We needed a framework, not a guess, not a marketing line, but a science-based method to measure the climate impact of our portfolio and to help us understand which sectors and clients needed our support in their transition. So we built one.

"We didn't start with the full bank. We started with the sectors that had the highest carbon intensity, energy, heavy industry, housing, and we worked with third-party experts to build the methodology from the ground up. We asked: What's the current footprint of what we finance? What's the pathway to get to 1.5 degrees? How can we help our clients decarbonize?

"That's what the Terra Approach became: a way to actively manage our portfolio to protect our clients and ourselves against climate risks, not by divesting but by engaging. By using the power of our financing to support the transition, rather than walk away from it. That's impact at scale. And that's the role we saw for ING and still see."

—LEON WIJNANDS, ING HEAD OF SUSTAINABILITY

OWNING THE FLIP SIDE

When I first became CEO, I said in an interview with former BBC journalist René Carayol that we had to earn back society's trust,[8] which meant recognizing not just the upside of our actions but also the unintended consequences. That awareness became the foundation for the Think Forward Initiative, as previously described.

As a true purpose-driven organization, we had to understand the full impact of our success. That's also where our sustainability strategy took shape. We knew that financing large companies could drive economic growth, but we also had to acknowledge the other side: a significant carbon footprint. Real transformation meant being honest about both sides of the equation and building a strategy that could deliver value without compromise.

BANKING ON CLIMATE: THE PRECURSOR TO TERRA

We explored how to be both effective and science-based in the fight against global warming at the start. Of course, we're a commercial institution; one of our roles is to support economic growth. It's what banks are meant to do. With that role comes responsibility; however, we had to remain conscious of the environment.

One way to address that is through exclusion or setting strict policies about what you will and won't finance. For instance, most banks avoided certain arms industries, positioning themselves as forces for peace. At ING, we were very selective in financing the arms industry. Now we're criticized for that decision, but I can tell you, eight years ago, had we actively financed certain arms producers, we might have lost windows in our headquarters, literally. Activists would've vandalized the building, just as they do today in response to oil and gas financing.

We also ruled out coal. In December 2017, we announced that if a power company generated more than 5 percent of its capacity from coal-fired plants, and they would not show us a plan to reduce it to below 5 percent by 2025, we exited the relationship. We would ask our client to look for another bank, close accounts, and get refinanced. That's exclusion. It sends a message. While it may be principled, it isn't always constructive or effective.

Exclusion is currently leading to other banks and private credit funds financing exactly those companies but without having the conversation how to change in line with the Paris Accord.

Exclusion draws a line. It says what you won't support, but it doesn't help the system evolve. Evolution, not isolation, is what drives lasting change.

OUR GERMAN POWER COMPANY CHALLENGE

One of the most defining examples of putting our sustainability strategy into action came with a major German energy company. At the time, more than 5 percent of their power generation came from coal. We sent them a letter stating that unless they presented a science-based and credible plan to bring that number below 5 percent, we would need to reconsider our relationship.

They were outraged. "How can a bank tell us how to run our business?" they asked.

We stood firm and made it clear: "This is how we operate. There are other banks, and you're free to seek financing elsewhere. If you don't reduce your coal exposure below the threshold, we won't be able to continue financing you."

BEYOND EXCLUSION: THE TERRA
APPROACH FRAMEWORK

The more constructive approach, the one we ultimately pursued, was to develop a framework that could help the industry change. That's what made the Terra Approach so powerful. It wasn't about divestment or saying no. It was about enabling transformation.

The breakthrough came when we figured out how to measure the full carbon impact of our loan book, specifically Scope 3 emissions. It took time to find the right external partners and agencies who had developed the science-based methodologies necessary to do this credibly.

To understand the significance:

- Scope 1 covers emissions from a source directly controlled by ING, like usage of natural gas, heating oil, and diesel.
- Scope 2 includes indirect emissions from the energy or products a company purchases, such as electricity, paper, or water. These can often be influenced by selecting sustainable providers or demanding higher standards from vendors.
- Scope 3 is where it gets complex. These are the emissions caused by the company's use of business travel but also broader activities through its value chain, products, or services. For banks, that includes the carbon footprint of the sectors and companies we finance. If we lend to a steel manufacturer or finance a house, part of this footprint would be attributed to ING.

Although Scopes 1 and 2 are rather limited for banks, we came out with very strict targets for ourselves. We needed to deliver on those targets to credibly steer Scope 3. Scope 3 is where banks can make a difference.

The largest carbon footprint in the world today comes from the residential housing sector, because of poor insulation, inefficient heating systems, and outdated infrastructure. That's not a popular topic for politicians, though. Few are eager to campaign on replacing insulation. Other major emitters are, for example, the cement industry, automotive, oil and gas, transportation, shipping, and aviation. Banks finance all of them.

The question we had to ask ourselves was this: *if we're financing the industries driving global emissions, how can we help change that, rather than exclude them?* The Terra Approach became our answer.

THE TERRA BREAKTHROUGH

We developed the Terra Approach, a transformative way to calculate our indirect carbon footprint based on what we financed. Take a loan to an oil and gas company for example. Under Terra, we would attribute a share of its total emissions to our financing, proportional to the size of our loan. That portion became our ambition to reduce it.

This was a breakthrough because we didn't rely on assumptions or internal estimates. We built this approach on science-based targets, using independently verified methodologies from leading environmental agencies like the 2 Degrees Investing Initiative. These frameworks allowed us to credibly calculate the emissions linked to our loan portfolio across industries.

Let's say our total loan book to the oil and gas sector was €10 billion. If that equated to a footprint of ten, we'd publicly commit to reducing the emission intensity of that loan book to a certain level over the next thirty years. The reduction had to be science-based and in line with the Paris Accord.

Terra offered a strategic alternative to exclusion: engage our clients, support their transition, and help finance the shift toward lower-emission business models. It wasn't about shrinking the loan book; it was about reducing the emission intensity of it.

CONSTRUCTIVE ENGAGEMENT

Rather than simply walking away from high-emitting sectors, we chose to engage. That was the real power of the Terra Approach. We sat down with clients, especially those in carbon-intensive industries and said, "There are new technologies, new energy sources, and more sustainable ways to operate. If you're willing to invest in them, we're willing to help finance that transition."

More than that, often we offered a tangible incentive like better financing terms. If clients committed to investing in greener technologies, we would offer discounts on our margins. It was a practical way to align our clients' transformation with our purpose and to put real weight behind our commitments.

We started with just a few key sectors: residential real estate, commercial real estate, power generation, automotive, and cement. We launched the program at the COP24 climate conference in Katowice in 2018, where we pledged to reduce the Scope 3 emissions of these lending portfolios by a specific percentage over time.

Since then, the Terra Approach has expanded across nearly all major portfolios. Here's the most important part: we made it fully transparent. Each year, ING publicly reports whether it has met, exceeded, or fallen short of its Terra targets, portfolio by portfolio. That level of accountability was rare in the industry, but we believed it was necessary.

The Terra Approach wasn't just about measurement. It was

about steering, and it reflected a shift in how we saw our role, not as passive financiers but as active partners in the transition to a more sustainable economy.

THE DANCING FOOL: LEADING INDUSTRY CHANGE

At the time, it was unheard of for banks to take a public stance like this, to say, "If we can't reduce our clients' carbon footprint, we'll reduce our loan portfolio."

Our first goal wasn't to shrink the loan book; it was to help our clients decarbonize and thus be future-proof. The solution didn't matter as much as the direction, magnitude, and timing. The point was you can stay a step ahead in life and in business but only if you're honest about the harm your business causes and willing to take that seriously.

Also in that respect, you needed to stay a step ahead.

That was the deeper purpose behind Terra. We made it clear: we would hold our clients accountable, just as we do ourselves.

Being the first to take a bold step like this comes with risk, however. I've often compared it to that video of a music festival where one person starts dancing, wildly, awkwardly, completely alone. People stare. Then, someone else joins in. Then another. Eventually, everyone is dancing. That's how movements start.

ING was that first dancer. We launched the Terra Approach knowing it would be controversial. To make it stick, we needed others to join us. Ahead of the Katowice COP24 climate conference, where global leaders and UN Secretary General, Antonio Guterres, would be present, we deliberately positioned ourselves as a coalition of the willing. BNP Paribas, Société Générale, BBVA, and Standard Chartered joined ING in making similar pledges together, aligning a combined loan book of €2.4 trillion with global climate goals. This collective pledge became known as the Katowice Commitment. These banks chose to move first, not because they were forced to but because they believed responsibility and competitiveness could go hand in hand.

It was rare (almost unheard of) for direct competitors to align this way.

Yet they did.

Four other banks agreed to follow our lead. That collective signal mattered. It turned a single initiative into a shared movement, and it made clear that this was not about ING standing apart but about reshaping expectations for the industry.

FROM TERRA TO NET ZERO

That was the moment everyone started dancing. We had been the fool, the first one to stand up and say, "We're going to make this commitment." Inside the commercial organization of the wholesale bank, many thought we were crazy.

"We're going to lose all our clients," they said. "How can we possibly pull this off?"

It was the leadership of the wholesale bank that initiated it, though. I remember during one of our top 200 gatherings, one of the wholesale bank leaders gave a deeply inspiring and emotional speech about the impact of global warming. The room fell silent as he described, with conviction, just how damaging it was becoming. He was the daring one, the one with foresight.

We stuck to our vision, and then something remarkable happened: other banks started following.

The Net Zero movement was the natural evolution of the Terra Approach. From the first five banks (including ING), it took just a year or two for a much larger group, representing nearly a third of all global banking assets, to sign a collective pledge. Each bank committed to managing its lending portfolio in line with the Paris Accord.

What does that mean in practice? The Paris Accord's central goal is clear: total net carbon emissions must reach zero by 2050. That doesn't mean eliminating all carbon-producing activities; it means balancing them out with carbon-reducing ones. In other words, for every ton of emissions, you must support an equivalent ton of carbon capture or reduction. That's the essence of "net zero."

This led to a wave of commitments: the Net Zero Banking Alliance, the Net Zero Asset Managers initiative, and others. The corporate leaders took their responsibility.

WHEN BUSINESS LEADS WHERE POLITICS CAN'T

To truly address today's societal and environmental challenges, companies must take a holistic approach. For example: the growing gap between the wealthy and the poor is eroding the middle class, a group that historically served as a stabilizing force in society. The middle class believed they had a fair shot at success, which kept them engaged and anchored in moderate politics.

That stability has faded. As polarization has increased, so has disillusionment. Political leaders, faced with fractured electorates, have struggled to build consensus around the bold actions required to create a better world. The initiatives that matter most, like environmental sustainability or social equity, often come with a price tag too high for widespread political support.

That's where corporate leaders have stepped in. While politicians are caught up in debate, business leaders have been able to move. Governments' stance and policies have not been stable long term. Which is needed. Companies, however, have embraced these challenges not just as obligations but as opportunities to lead with purpose, to innovate, and to create long-term value.

THE BOARDROOM CHALLENGE

Our story starts with purpose, but when you reach the level of societal impact, it's no longer about what you say; it's about what you *do.* Many organizations rely on polished narratives and well-designed campaigns, but for us, it was about putting our full capabilities to work. Terra was a prime example: rooted in core banking but bold in its innovation. That's what it means to serve society, not just by speaking about the environment but by acting on it.

It took over a year of intense internal work to build the Terra Approach, something science-based, a plan the market could believe in, that we could execute, and that wouldn't fall apart under pressure. We knew critics were watching. We also knew that if we weren't serious, if we couldn't measure it, track it, and report on it, we would be contributing to the very problem we were trying to solve: greenwashing.

That same mindset informed our role in advancing the Principles for Responsible Banking. In 2019, we presented the initiative at the United Nations to formally launch it on a global stage. At the time, this was not just an ING position: it represented a coalition of more than 130 banks, accounting for roughly one-third of the global banking industry.

I spoke on behalf of that group at the UN, making the case that banks could no longer treat sustainability as an add-on or a communications exercise. The principles were a collective commitment to align banking with society's goals and to be transparent about progress and trade-offs. What mattered most was not that ING helped initiate the effort but that competitors chose to stand alongside us. That level of alignment signaled a shift in expectations for the industry.

While those principles aligned with Terra's sustainability mission, they extended far beyond it, embedding purpose into broader business practices.

We were committing to action rooted in reality.

That's what it means to live your purpose. Not just to write one.

UN SUSTAINABLE DEVELOPMENT GOALS

Like many companies, we eventually aligned our commitments to the United Nations' Sustainable Development Goals (SDGs), using them as a compass to identify the areas where we could make a meaningful, transparent contribution.

The SDGs provided a common language and structure, allowing companies across industries and borders to anchor their efforts in shared global priorities. Whether it was climate action, inclusive economic growth, or gender equality, the SDGs helped translate purpose into focus. For ING, the Terra Approach mapped closely to goals related to climate action (SDG 13) and responsible production and consumption (SDG 12). The Think Forward Initiative contributed toward sustainable and inclusive economic growth (SDG 8) and reduced inequalities (SDG 10).

None of these initiatives were overnight efforts. The Think Forward Initiative started in late 2015. The Terra Approach was conceived in 2017–2018.

The development of the Terra Approach, spearheaded by Leon Wijnands, ING Head of Sustainability, was a journey of discovery. We began with an open mind, exploring where the narrative would lead. But this initiative required so much foundational change, culture, structure, and sector knowledge that it took time before we could fully operationalize it.

REGAINING TRUST IS NOT EASY

Thinking and acting from purpose while genuinely taking societal responsibilities into account is not easy. Every decision has multiple dimensions and affects different stakeholders, all of whom must be considered. As described earlier, ING focused on areas where we believed we could make a meaningful contribution to society: improving financial literacy, helping people become more financially self-reliant, and addressing climate change through our loan portfolio. These efforts are about building a strong, well-performing company; they are essential to curating trust in society.

Remember...trust arrives on foot and leaves on horseback.

That trust was severely tested on September 4, 2018, when ING entered a settlement with the Dutch Public Prosecution

Office and paid a total fine of €775 million. While our strategy was delivering results and our focus on rebuilding trust was genuine and sustained, we failed in one critical area.

Banks have a clear responsibility to protect the financial system from financial and economic crime. A two-year investigation by the Dutch Public Prosecution Office concluded that the processes and procedures at ING Netherlands did not meet expectations. We were found to have underinvested in systems and people to prevent money laundering. That conclusion was a major blow to the reputation we had worked so hard to rebuild.

I had celebrated our progress with colleagues in good times. In this moment, I had to stand just as visibly in front of them when we were publicly criticized. I informed colleagues across the world directly, through video messages, and addressed the issue publicly as well, through a press release, interviews in the Dutch media, and an apology in the Dutch Parliament.

I personally took responsibility for leading the improvement and remediation program. It was essential to demonstrate that this was a matter of global importance for ING. Trust that had been painstakingly rebuilt after the financial crisis, particularly in the Netherlands, now had to be rebuilt again.

Compliance and risk programs we had already initiated in 2015 needed to be strengthened and intensified. Our goal was not only to remediate past shortcomings but to ensure that the learnings were embedded in our behavior and risk culture going forward.

This comprehensive, global improvement program had a significant impact on employee engagement. The broader transformation continued, but in our QBRs, we deliberately allocated additional technology and human resources to strengthen our compliance efforts.

For some time, it remained the primary topic of the Leadership Council's quarterly agenda, and we structured our upcoming top 200 gathering around this priority. We examined our strengths and distinctive capabilities to determine how we could accelerate progress. Our Accelerator Labs developed new compliance technology solutions, including digital Customer Due Diligence (CDD) and enhanced transaction monitoring.

The centralization and standardization we had implemented earlier were now proving their value, enabling us to monitor and roll out new regulatory requirements globally and more efficiently, not only in KYC/AML but also in areas such as MiFID and GDPR.

Remediation alone is never enough. You have to make systems, processes, and mindsets future-proof. Regulations continue to evolve, expectations change, and new technologies emerge. In that environment, maintaining an effective gatekeeper role requires constant focus and sustained investment.

WHERE IMPACT BEGINS

Purpose is a lens, a compass, and a commitment to show up, even when it's hard, even when you're the first one dancing.

At ING, we began with something simple: empowering people stay a step ahead in life and in business. That clarity gave us the courage to ask harder questions.

1. What role should we play in society?
2. What consequences do we own, intended or not?
3. How can we lead where politics stalls?

The answers led us to reimagine our business from the inside out, from digital innovation to climate accountability, from culture to capital.

We didn't wait for consensus. We acted, partnered, and led. In doing so, we showed what's possible when business becomes a force for lasting good.

One of the hardest lessons of impact at scale is this: even with the best intentions, you can still disappoint. Large institutions operate under intense scrutiny, and outcomes are judged not only by intent but by impact. Decisions made to stabilize systems, protect customers, or resolve past issues can still leave people feeling let down or unheard. That tension does not disappear simply because the rationale is sound. Impact at scale means accepting that responsibility does not end when you believe you have done the right thing: it extends to understanding how those actions are experienced and being willing to stand in that discomfort.

READING THE TEA LEAVES

The role companies play is changing, just as regulatory and societal expectations are changing. As a result, past decisions are increasingly judged with the benefit of hindsight, or against moral and ethical standards that did not exist at the time. Leading a global institution has never been simple, but anticipating future change and making the right decisions in that context has become increasingly difficult.

Take decisions around reducing the carbon footprint of a loan portfolio. You may be applauded for taking action. At the same time, activists may criticize you for not moving fast enough, while governments in regions dependent on fossil fuels may respond with boycotts or political pressure. There is no single truth and no universally right path. In the end, as a leader, you must decide what you believe is right and accept the consequences of that choice. What matters is that the decision is made with the right intentions, rooted in customer interests, and clearly explained. Contexts change over time, but climate change is real. Corporate leaders must stand for what they believe in, even when it is uncomfortable.

At the same time, societal expectations themselves can shift, and sometimes very quickly. Where ING once had clear policies not to finance the arms industry or nuclear power, by 2025, we saw politicians and society increasingly expecting the opposite. Rising geopolitical tensions have pushed many countries to strengthen their defense capabilities and reduce their dependence on other nations for energy and critical resources. We are moving away from a fully globalized world toward a more fragmented, tri-polar one, where self-sufficiency and security have become priorities.

UBS has described this as the "decade of security": food security, energy security, and physical and cyber security. In such a context, activities once viewed as immoral or unethical can suddenly be framed as a moral responsibility, such as financing parts of the defense industry. Banks inevitably have a role to play, but it must be a careful one. As with financial and economic crime, the expectation is not that banks fight these issues themselves but that they help protect society from them.

Given these shorter political and government policy cycles, purpose becomes even more important. Staying true to your purpose while adjusting tactics to a changing environment helps leaders continue to find their way. Impact only comes when actions are clearly connected to what matters to clients. Acting with the best intentions for society may resonate for a time, but it can just as quickly be turned against you.

Leaders must continue to *read the tea leaves*: navigate a rapidly changing world order and shifting stakeholder expectations while ensuring that their actions remain aligned with their purpose and are grounded in client relevance. That is how leadership remains authentic, credible, and impactful.

The questions we faced around sustainability and societal impact were not unique. They were early signals of a broader shift: leadership in an era of accelerating complexity. Just as digital once reshaped banking, a new wave of technological acceleration is now forcing leaders to confront the same fundamental questions again, only faster and at a greater scale.

CHAPTER 11

THE NEXT FRONTIER

Artificial intelligence marks another inflection point in business history. Like digital before it, AI will not wait for consensus. Organizations that adapt boldly, guided by purpose and disciplined execution, will turn disruption into advantage; those that hesitate will be defined by it. The same framework that guided ING's transformation—anchoring in purpose with a clear customer proposition and aligning leadership, culture, capabilities, and incentives to support a consistent strategy execution—can help leaders navigate this next wave. AI may be new, but the discipline required to transform around it is not.

The first time I was shown Arta Finance's AI agents, it wasn't framed as a demo.

Caesar Sengupta, Co-founder and CEO of Arta Finance, had asked if I wanted to see what they were building. He had spent years at Google, led Google Pay and Google Finance, and now he was rebuilding private banking from the ground up with an AI-first wealth platform. I had agreed to advise the company because the ambition felt familiar: not incremental improvement but a rethinking of what the system was for.

He introduced two agents: one designed to act as a product specialist, the other as an investment specialist.

Caesar watched me closely as they ran.

"This is still early," he said. "But this is the direction."

I nodded, then asked my first questions.

"What role is each agent playing, and where does it stop?"

He smiled. "That's exactly the right question."

We talked through the architecture. Where the data came from, how context was framed, and where human judgment re-entered the loop. I wasn't interested in whether the agents sounded fluent. Fluency is easy. I wanted to know how they behaved under pressure.

"What happens," I asked, "when the model is confident but wrong?"

"That's the risk," Caesar said. "And it's why we're being very deliberate."

Over the next few weeks, we kept returning to the same themes. Not hype. Not speed for its own sake. Discipline.

"How do you prevent this from becoming a black box?" I asked him at one point.

"You design it so it can't be one," he said.

"We're building an AI wealth company to reinvent private banking from scratch. A lot of what we do is AI-first: AI agents at the bleeding edge of how to use AI in wealth. What's rare, and what made Ralph so valuable to us, is that he combines real depth in banking and wealth with an intuitive understanding of technology, including the regulatory constraints."

—CAESAR SENGUPTA, CO-FOUNDER AND FORMER CEO, ARTA FINANCE

AI rewards seriousness. It punishes vagueness. The organizations that rush toward it without deciding what they expect from it, or what they will not allow it to do, will be disappointed. The ones that treat it as a capability to be shaped, tested, and constrained will move faster and safer.

What impressed me most wasn't the technology itself. It was the posture behind it. Clear roles. Explicit boundaries. A refusal to confuse intelligence with judgment.

I had seen this before.

At ING, digital transformation succeeded not because we chased new tools but because we were explicit about delivering a frictionless customer experience, using the latest technology. AI raises the stakes, but the underlying challenge is the same. Decisions compound faster. Mistakes travel further. Leadership is tested earlier. So what do you want to use it for, and how do you set the right direction?

That is why so many leaders now ask me about ING's transformation. They are not looking for predictions about AI. They are looking for a way to think clearly under pressure.

THE PRESSURES OF AN AI ERA

I left ING to join UBS in 2020, but it is interesting to recognize how many requests I received in *2024 and 2025* to explain ING's transformation story. I have been asked to explain:

- How we saw the disruption and opportunity of digital,
- Why we saw this as an opportunity rather than a threat, and
- Why we transformed so deeply and thoroughly.

I have stood in front of hundreds of executives over the years, walking them through our transformation story with all its successes and shortcomings. By the time we reach the Q&A, their real interest becomes clear: they want to understand what our journey means for their own organizations as they confront the possibilities and pressures of the AI era. Those conversations, and the questions behind them, are ultimately why I decided to write this book.

Apart from telling an interesting journey, this book offers lessons for every executive. Especially now, as many are grappling with what the rise of AI means for their own industries, our story shows what a full and comprehensive transformation at ING required. At the time, and given our DNA, digital felt far more like an opportunity than anything else. In our discussions in 2013 and 2014, we already sensed that this was more than a tactical shift; it was a genuine strategic inflection point.

Of course, I have my own views on AI: how it may develop, which industries it could reshape, and how society might be affected. The pace of change is so fast, however, that by the time this book reaches your desk or coffee table, those views may already be outdated. That's why this is not about predicting how AI will unfold or prescribing how you should respond. Instead, it is meant to help you make your own assessment of AI's impact, using parallels from ING's transformation journey to guide your thinking.

THE RELEVANCE OF ING'S TRANSFORMATION IN THE AGE OF AI

As we look toward the future, the broader conversation about transformation will inevitably return, this time centered on AI. We're standing at the edge of another wave of massive, multi-level change.

ING's strategy was reshaped to account for digital, so the

parallels are clear. But simply remember that AI won't change your purpose, assuming you've defined one. AI doesn't alter the fundamental reason an organization exists. However, AI can change the strategy. If it impacts the core of what the company does, then it must be addressed. If AI is influencing the business that deeply, this book is highly relevant.

On the other hand, if AI is primarily a tool your company uses to boost productivity or defend existing positions, then the lessons here may not apply as directly.

The red thread running through this book is if you remain anchored in your purpose and approach change with the right mindset and method, you'll be able to navigate what's ahead. AI disruption isn't slowing down. It's accelerating.

AI: THREAT OR OPPORTUNITY?

At some point, every leader faces the same fundamental question when confronted with a new technology: is this a threat or an opportunity?

If it's a threat, is it existential? Does it challenge the core of your business model? Or is it a more contained threat to a single product, service, or capability?

If it's an opportunity, is it tactical, offering a marginal competitive advantage? Or is it strategic, something that could accelerate your development and position you as a leader in your industry?

Some will see AI more as a defensive movement, a challenge they need to respond to to protect what they have. Others will see it as an offensive movement, viewing it as a chance to build new side businesses or create strategic opportunities, like we did with ING.

Even if you see AI as a strategic opportunity, without a

motivating vision and a compelling story, you won't bring your people with you. Remember the burning ambition versus burning platform? Without this, the necessary transformation doesn't stand a chance.

Transformation focuses on a simple but profound truth: change is never truly finished, and the rise of artificial intelligence marks a new inflection point for business transformation. As organizations face faster, deeper, more disruptive waves of change than ever before, the lesson remains the same…adapt boldly, disrupt yourself, or risk irrelevance.

The foundation of this entire approach echoes Darwin's principle: in times of constant change, survival doesn't favor the strongest or the most intelligent; it favors those who adapt. That's why transformation is essential and why leaders must stay at the forefront of emerging developments and assess them with clarity.

BANKING'S EVOLUTION: FROM AUTOMATION TO HUMAN CONNECTION

"What stood out to me was that Ralph could look five years ahead and translate a vision and its enablers (digital then, AI now) into plain language that landed with people: what it meant for them, how it could make their lives easier, and why it could feel insecure. Because AI creates uncertainty, and in a human-capital environment like a bank, you don't win on numbers alone. You must address the human side as seriously as the business side."

—KLAAS WAGENAAR, CHAIRMAN, LEXGEN A.I.

Throughout my career, I've seen wave after wave of transformation in banking, each driven by new technologies that displaced or reshaped human roles.

It began with the automation of stock exchange settlements in the 1980s, followed by electronic payments. Paper-based transactions gave way to systems that could move money faster, more cheaply, and with greater accuracy. As banking operations became increasingly computerized, they also became more efficient.

Here's what's fascinating about digitalization: banks didn't just automate internal processes; we effectively outsourced work back to the client. In the past, a customer would write a check or fill out a paper form. That form would go to the bank, where a back-office employee would process it. Today, customers enter data themselves, initiate the transaction, and approve it.

Digital banking puts the customer in control, giving them transparency, immediacy, and convenience. From their perspective, the experience improved. But behind the scenes, banks offloaded significant operational work without outsourcing it externally. It was a subtle but powerful shift in how value was created and delivered.

The financial sector, both banking and insurance, will be able to implement AI faster and more effectively than many other industries. The digital era has already forced us to build strong data-management capabilities, and regulatory requirements around modeling, scoring, and discrimination mean we are better prepared for responsible and ethical AI adoption. Other sectors face a steeper learning curve. They will need significant investment in areas such as data quality, model governance, and compliance before they can benefit in the same way. That may slow them down and make them more vulnerable to new entrants, much as banks were when digital-driven fintechs first appeared. In banking, I believe AI will drive a fast evolutionary change rather than a revolutionary one. After decades of automation, the remaining value in banking lies in intelligence, places where human insight still matters, like parts of investment banking, asset management, and wealth management. Yet even this is beginning to change because of AI.

In corporate and investment banking, the role of the advisor often involves deep industry knowledge. Understanding sectors like oil and gas, telecom, media, or technology allows relationship managers to structure customized solutions. AI will enhance this type of work: accelerating knowledge gathering, surfacing insights, financial modeling, and valuations and enabling faster problem-solving and leveraging banking practices across industries. It won't fully replace it. I believe that instead AI will raise the productivity of analysts and advisors, not eliminate them.

The investment profession, and the investment advice profession in particular, stands to benefit enormously if AI is applied well. With the right underlying data, AI will enable stronger portfolio management and more personalized, needs-driven investment strategies for individual clients.

These are games of numbers, optimizing investment portfolios, managing time horizons, and evaluating risks across numerically endless possibilities. It's an area where AI will outperform humans in calculating what is best. The complexity and scale of that decision-making process make it ideal for machine learning and algorithmic recommendations. Here, we'll see major disruption as AI tools outperform traditional advisors in speed, precision, and customization.

WILL AI EVER BE ABLE TO CARE LIKE HUMANS?

AI increasingly thinks like humans and speaks like humans, but will it ever care like humans?

We already see a wave of specialized scale-ups emerging in this space. Some provide tailored AI tools that support investment advisers and self-directed investors with notifications about changes. Others offer a fully digital wealth-management experience, giving individuals access to products and services that were once available only to the very wealthy yet without a human adviser involved. These applications generate advice, communicate directly with the user, and are evolving rapidly toward something that feels remarkably close to a human interaction. The tone, the language, the responsiveness all appear human.

The real question is whether empathy and trust can be replicated or whether they become less important as people grow more comfortable with the recommendations these systems provide. AI can already reach out around key trigger moments: market movements, new information that contradicts your assumptions, or changes in your personal financial situation.

Trust in these applications can be built over time. Is this at the same level as human trust, though?

IS THE HUMAN ELEMENT IRREPLACEABLE?

Human connection, empathy, and relational depth remain central to certain types of advice, particularly financial decisions that intersect with personal identity, life milestones, and emotional stakes.

Consider the scenario: "I have $100,000 in my private pension plan (or 401[k]). My kids are heading to college soon. What should I do?" This is not just a mathematical optimization problem. It's a deeply personal decision involving fears, hopes, values, and long-term goals. It also has different solutions.

As I've said, AI already handles the analytics better than any human. It can evaluate scenarios, surface options, and even hold a coherent conversation about possible solutions.

However, trust does not emerge from analytics alone.

Over time, nudges, notifications, and consistent recommendations may teach people to rely on an algorithm and believe it is doing a good job. That kind of functional trust will grow. Yet deeper trust, the kind that makes people feel safe, understood, and genuinely cared for, is rooted in human concepts: altruism, judgment, responsibility, and care.

Human understanding, emotional nuance, and the space to feel heard still belong to us. In an age of automation, those who can combine intelligent systems with genuine human connection will matter more than ever, not despite AI but because of it.

THE MORTGAGE PARADOX: TRUST AND DECEPTION

For most people, buying a home, and taking on a mortgage, is the single biggest financial decision of their lives. It involves significant long-term debt, yet many make this commitment without fully understanding fundamental concepts like compound interest or risk over time.

This creates a paradox. In these high-stakes situations, consumers often rely on people they trust, like mortgage brokers, bank representatives, and financial advisors. That trust can be reassuring, but it does not always equate to good advice. Aside from the fact that it can leave people vulnerable to manipulation.

Humans make mistakes every day. They misjudge, overlook details, and bring emotion and incentives into decisions that should be objective. Yet we tend to accept those imperfections.

With AI, the expectation is often different. Many people say, "I could never trust an algorithm with financial advice," as if perfection were the baseline requirement. That raises an important question: *why do we expect AI to be flawless when we have always accepted fallibility in human judgment?*

The real challenge, then, is not choosing between humans or machines. It is understanding where each is strong and where each is weak, and how the combination can lead to an improvement from today's practice.

For the financial world, the technical solution lays in using deterministic models, using convex optimizations with LLMs, to come to the best solution/advice.

The quality and reliability of the LLMs used in AI agents to understand a customer's need can be improved by reusing mechanisms that were developed for training, evaluating, and ensuring the quality of, by definition nondeterministic, humans performing a task.

This combination reduces mistakes and improves the quality and consistency of advice beyond what a normal advisor can perform and leaves the option of delivering the advice to the customer between a human advisor or a virtual (AI) advisor.

A RADICAL ACCELERATION

Some jobs will undoubtedly be displaced. More often, however, I believe we'll see a radical acceleration in how quickly conclusions are reached and outputs are delivered. Many industries, once buffered from disruption, will be now experiencing what banking went through during its digital transformation.

Like banking, they'll need to evolve or risk being left behind.

If companies respond too defensively, they will almost certainly be disrupted. But if they embrace the opportunities AI creates, the picture looks very different. Yes, some jobs will disappear. Yet, as we saw in banking, AI also makes it possible to deliver high-quality practices and advice—once reserved for larger, wealthier clients—to much smaller clients as well. The democratization of high-quality advice and service in, for example, legal, tax and accounting industries is a real business opportunity. It expands access, creates new demand, and ultimately generates new jobs. This upside is available only to the first movers.

REACTION OF THE INTELLECTUAL ELITE

I've noticed something ironic: many of the people who once felt intellectually untouchable, confident their roles would never be disrupted, are now the ones questioning progress.

Historically, these people were quick to justify industrial and technological change. When jobs were lost to automation or to new tools, from horse-drawn plows to tractors, from handwritten ledgers to digital spreadsheets, they'd say, "That's just progress." They encouraged others to adapt, retrain, and accept disruption as a fact of life.

Now that their roles are being challenged, whether by AI writing scripts, producing films, or automating legal or financial work, they're the ones calling for protection.

For centuries, they believed others should not complain. Change was inevitable. Skills had to evolve. Now that the disruption is at their own doorstep, the reaction is different.

It's a familiar pattern: when survival feels distant, it's easy to be objective. When your own relevance is questioned, the fear becomes personal. That's when the true test of adaptability begins.

And now it applies to us.

For decades, many highly educated professionals could

remain somewhat distant from the underlying mechanics of technological change. They benefited from digitalization but rarely had to deeply understand it. AI is different. It reaches into the core of knowledge and creative work itself, which means even those who once felt insulated now have to engage more directly with the technology shaping their field.

I can relate to that shift. It's not comfortable when the ground moves beneath your own expertise. But that's exactly why we have to examine how our adaptability can create opportunity. Every profession can benefit from AI if we are willing to embrace it thoughtfully. It can improve both productivity and the quality of our work.

Beyond that, as with highly specialized products and advice, AI creates the possibility, even the opportunity, to extend our reach to a broader customer base or audience, democratizing access to expertise that was once limited to a few.

SETTING BOUNDARIES: THE ETHICAL IMPERATIVE

Very few industries will emerge untouched by AI, simply because it is so much more efficient at so many tasks. The risk comes when people put too much faith in it. AI should be treated as a tool, something to be cross-checked, not trusted to be 100 percent accurate all the time. Like human beings, analysis or decision-making is not always 100 percent right. Don't expect this from AI, but don't make it an excuse for not using it either.

There are several areas where we need to protect ourselves from AI going too far. First and foremost is setting boundaries around outcomes, recommendations, and self-learning to prevent bias.

It's easy for AI to become biased. At the end of the day, these are still computer programs. If the answer is X once, then X again, and then X a third time, the system begins to treat X as truth. X may not be true, however.

The key is to support AI's development in a way that is safe, especially in terms of ethical standards. The definition of what's ethical is evolving rapidly, and AI itself is accelerating that evolution. During the periods when society considers something unethical, there must be clear laws, regulations, and audit mechanisms to ensure AI is applied responsibly. This includes monitoring for bias, discrimination, and unintended consequences. Start with a clear ethical framework. Safe and responsible application is essential, and you simply cannot afford mistakes here. Even in an era of constant change, one thing doesn't change: trust comes on foot and leaves on horseback. So err on the side of conservatism here.

One can draw a parallel here: just like we train and coach human beings on nondeterministic elements, we can do the same with AI. One can incorporate human feedback and expertise, implement self-supervised and active learning, emulate human thought-processes, implement verification layers to double check, curate data, etc.

AN ECHO CHAMBER EFFECT

Another risk, which might seem benign on the surface, is how AI can make us less informed. Because AI learns your preferences, it starts feeding you answers you're likely to agree with, not necessarily answers that broaden your thinking.

It's a fascinating contradiction. We now have access to more information than ever before, yet we can tailor that information so precisely that we end up narrowing our worldview. AI enables confirmation bias at scale. This is why it's so important to cross-check outputs, run prompts through multiple models, and ask different types of questions. Navigating AI effectively is becoming a discipline of its own.

So, if you sense resistance in your organization around AI, listen carefully. The impact of it is fundamentally different from earlier technological disruptions. It introduces a wider range of ethical considerations that must be addressed before you can deploy it at scale.

- Enterprise AI gives you more oversight and control.
- Sector-specific AI allows for tighter verification because it is designed around the realities of a particular industry.
- Specialist AI goes even further, trained for highly specific tasks such as tax or accounting advice.

Equally important is ensuring that the people who use your AI systems are properly trained. They need to understand how to prompt effectively; how to assign the AI agent a clear role, define its task, provide the right context, and specify the expected output. When they do this well, the risk of hallucination becomes far more manageable. As a guiding rule, the HILTI principle remains essential: Human-In-The-Loop Technology Integration.

THE DATA QUALITY CHALLENGE

Beyond ethics, there's another critical boundary: data quality. We must ensure that AI generates diverse recommendations and that the data used to generate them is clean and reliable.

Even if the algorithm is well-regulated and ethically sound, poor data can still produce dangerous or misleading outcomes. That's why the data sources behind AI must be audited, especially in industries where decisions carry real impact. This is where enterprise AI and specialized AI comes in: owning/knowing the data underlying the AI recommendation.

Ethical standards must be audited, too. Back-testing models must happen regularly. And your people must continue to take ownership of the outcome.

This is already standard practice in the banking industry: we're used to regulation. As AI becomes more pervasive, other sectors may need similar oversight, particularly when applying AI at scale.

HOW TO APPLY THE FRAMEWORK IN THE AGE OF AI

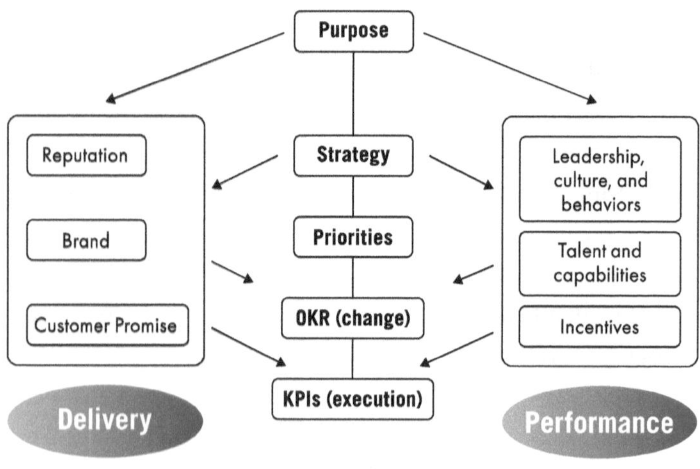

Returning to the framework and applying it to the AI challenge (or any disruptive industry trend) requires discipline across two dimensions: vertical alignment (from aspiration to execution) and horizontal alignment (from delivery to performance drivers).

DEVELOP THE VERTICAL AXIS: FROM ASPIRATION TO EXECUTION

The vertical axis moves from intention to reality. Vertical clarity answers the questions where are we going, and why?

1. Define Your Purpose

If your company does not yet have a clear purpose, define one. Anchor it in your historical strengths (your organizational DNA) especially those that proved resilient in difficult periods. Keep it concise and distinctive. It should not attempt to be everything to everyone, but it must be recognizable and energizing for those who need to act on it.

Most importantly, test it against real business dilemmas. If it does not guide difficult trade-offs, it is not yet strong enough.

2. Translate AI into Strategic Advantage

Assess what AI truly means for your business. Is it incremental, or does it challenge your core model? Decide deliberately how you want to use AI to differentiate: better advice, deeper insight, superior creativity, faster execution, productivity gains, or the ability to scale high-value services to broader audiences. Do not limit your inspiration to direct competitors. If you want to leapfrog, look outside your industry.

3. Set Clear Priorities and Execution Metrics

Once strategic choices are made, translate them into execution discipline. Define priorities. Establish OKRs and KPIs that make progress measurable.

DEVELOP THE HORIZONTAL AXIS: FROM DELIVERY TO PERFORMANCE DRIVERS

Clarity of direction alone is not enough. Many organizations fail not because their strategy was wrong but because their internal drivers were misaligned. That is where the horizontal axis comes in.

1. Define Your Customer Promise

Derive it directly from your purpose and strategy. Make it concrete enough that employees understand what must be delivered and can recognize their personal role in delivering it. AI can accelerate output, but it cannot replace clarity of promise.

2. Align Brand with Promise and Culture

Your brand must reinforce both your customer promise and your internal culture. Refresh or relaunch only when you are confident you can authentically deliver on what you communicate. A strong brand sharpens focus; a misaligned brand erodes trust.

3. Actively Manage Reputation

Move with ambition but not recklessness. Define zero-tolerance areas (ethical, regulatory, or societal) where mistakes are unacceptable. Anticipate unintended consequences of innovation and your success. Let purpose guide how you navigate the tensions AI introduces.

4. Assess Leadership, Talent, and Capabilities

Evaluate whether leaders truly have the conviction and capability to drive this change. Go beyond the executive team. Transformation requires depth. Tools such as the OHI can help assess whether management practices align with the archetype you aim to become.

5. Make Culture Observable and Accountable

Culture cannot remain abstract. Identify the behaviors that support successful execution, especially around accountability (given AI, more important than ever) and risk awareness (continue to look forward). Make them visible. Make them measurable. Consider embedding them into annual performance expectations.

6. Close the Capability Gap

Be honest about whether your culture and capabilities can sustain your ambition. If the gap is too large, adjust either the ambition or the investment in capabilities. Unrealistic stretch without support creates fatigue, not progress.

7. Cascade Performance and Incentives

Translate executive-level priorities into measurable targets throughout the organization. Cascade them as granularly as possible. Align incentives to reward not only results but the right behaviors that sustain long-term value.

8. Stay Consistent and Connect the Dots

During execution, maintain consistency of direction. Continuously connect the components of the framework. Use QBRs to zoom out (Are we still moving toward our strategic goal?) and zoom in (Are we adapting intelligently to short-term realities?).

AI will test organizations not only technologically but structurally. It will expose unclear purpose, magnify cultural weaknesses, and accelerate both good and bad execution.

The framework that guided ING through digital transformation does not prescribe what you should do with AI. It does something more important: it forces you to connect the dots deliberately, consistently, and continuously.

A NEW MANDATE FOR LEADERSHIP

We are once again at the edge of something profound. Artificial intelligence is not a temporary trend; it is a fundamental shift in how value is created, decisions are made, and trust is earned. Just like we did during ING's digital transformation, leaders must look beyond the tools themselves. You must explore AI, experiment with it, and embrace it. Also, ask harder questions:

- What does this trend mean in view of our purpose?
- Does our purpose give guidance around the use of AI?
- Can we use AI offensively, and if so, do we need to change our strategy?
- Will the speed and magnitude of change be evolutionary or revolutionary to us?

- What will it take to remain relevant, not just operationally but humanly?
- Can I refer to a burning platform in my organization, or should we transform from a burning ambition perspective?

The paradox of AI is that it forces us to become even more human. As algorithms handle the calculations, recommendations, and transactions, what remains is our capacity to connect, empathize, and lead. The real differentiator won't be speed, scale, or precision. It will be presence, judgment, and the ability to navigate complexity without losing clarity or conscience.

That's why transformation never ends. Every wave of change introduces new tools, new risks, and new opportunities.

The core challenge stays the same: don't wait to be disrupted, stay adaptable. But once you choose a clear direction, stay anchored in your purpose; connect the dots across strategy, customer promise, and culture; and remain consistent over time.

That is transformation.

CONCLUSION

The environment leaders operate in today is not simply more complex than it was a decade ago; it is more exposed. Decisions are made under public scrutiny, interpreted through shifting moral lenses, and reassessed long after the context that shaped them has faded. Intentions matter, but so does perception. Timing matters, but so does hindsight.

I learned this not from theory but from experience.

As CEO of a global institution, I often had to make decisions knowing they would be applauded by some and challenged by others, sometimes simultaneously. Whether the issue was climate policy, risk appetite, full digitalization of services, structural transformation, or cultural change, there was rarely a path that satisfied every stakeholder. Waiting for certainty was not an option. Acting without conviction was not responsible. Leadership lived in the space between the two.

THE TRANSFORMATION MOST LEADERS NOW FACE

Many of the leaders reading this book are standing in a similar moment. Artificial intelligence, digitalization, and new customer behaviors are not incremental forces; they are structural ones. They do not politely fit into existing organizations. They challenge how work is done, how value is created, and how responsibility is assigned.

What makes this moment particularly demanding is that transformation is happening on multiple levels at once. Technology is changing faster than culture. Expectations are shifting faster than practice. Practice is developing faster than regulation. Leaders are asked to make long-term commitments in an environment that rewards short-term reactions.

If this feels disorienting, it should. It is.

WAS IT WORTH IT?

Regularly, I get asked whether ING's comprehensive transformation delivered what we envisioned and whether the tremendous effort was worth it. In hindsight, one can never know what we might have accomplished had we chosen a different, possibly less ambitious direction.

ING's journey was one in which we sought to leapfrog from a financial conglomerate finalizing an immense restructuring to become the leading pan-European digital-primary bank. Looking at accelerated customer growth, the rapid increase in digital- and mobile-primary banking customers, the growth in cross-buy and fee-generating products (particularly visible in the last couple of years), and the industry-leading financial results in efficiency and returns during that period, we delivered on what we expected.

But did it unfold exactly as we imagined?

We saw the rise of neobanks becoming established names

like Monzo in the UK and Revolut across Europe, using standardized cross-border platform approaches. As we had anticipated, incumbents were massively disintermediated in payments through new modalities (such as QR) and new payment service providers combining these modalities, like Adyen and Stripe. Incumbents are now further challenged in lending by players like Klarna, YouLend, and GRAB, who deliver embedded finance in the online world.

So we were proven right in how we saw the future. The threat from fast-growing, technology-based challengers was (and still is) real. Despite their success, ING was able to credibly develop itself into a full-fledged digital-primary bank and find its own model to maintain direct, attractive relationships with customers. In many markets, ING is seen as one of the challengers rather than an incumbent.

The massive transformation, from a collection of country-specific banks with inconsistent brand promises, local and outdated technology, and fragmented products and customer experiences, has been successful. ING was able to standardize cross-border to the necessary degree in technology, data, risk management, and client experience. Service changes are now delivered quickly through a different way of working, creating a customer experience so intuitive that tens of millions of customers feel comfortable handling banking, with all its inherent complexity, themselves.

And finally, ING has been able to deliver exactly what it promises: Do Your Thing.

Did we succeed in everything? No. Did we succeed exactly as we thought we would? No. But that was inherent in the approach. An incumbent that draws inspiration from other industries in working practices, culture, and rapidly evolving technology must experiment, innovate, and learn from failure.

You should expect not to succeed in every area. And we did not. We failed in some. We failed fast. We fell, got up, learned, and moved forward. Without that, I am convinced we would not have changed so fundamentally, or so quickly. We would not be recognized as a leading pan-European digital-primary bank.

This book shows areas and practices in which we experimented and failed. That is precisely why I wrote it. As CEO, you must shape your strategy in light of your purpose, anticipate future trends, and see them as opportunities. You must hold conviction while remaining flexible in adapting to changing circumstances. The path is not straight. Adaptations can feel like failures…and sometimes they are. If you are not willing to accept that, do not begin an ambitious transformation.

Were we ever in doubt? Of course. We questioned the speed of the transformation and whether short-term course corrections were necessary. But we were never in doubt about the trends, their disruptive nature, or the need to act. Nor were we in doubt that ING, given its history and DNA in low-barrier banking and use of technology, was one of the few incumbents capable of taking this path.

Were we disappointed at times? Yes. We were disappointed by the limits of cross-border standardization and the resulting constraints on centralization. We were disappointed by the slow progress toward a fully realized European Banking Union.

But I was never disappointed in my colleagues. Not once. The journey was exciting for me and for them. It demanded reskilling and continuous learning. Some colleagues had to accept changes they did not welcome; some were asked to leave. But never did I feel disappointment in them. On the contrary.

From my perspective, the journey was worth it. It delivered a real-life, practice-tested framework for focused strategy execution and transformation. That is what this book is about.

Ultimately, I leave it to others to judge whether this comprehensive transformation was worth it to them. One can look at tangible commercial growth and financial results, at ING's digital banking capabilities, at its strengthened brand and culture, and objectively assess whether ING became a fundamentally different company than it was before.

WHY ING'S EXPERIENCE STILL MATTERS

ING's transformation did not begin with a technology road map. It began with a recognition that the organization had become too complex to serve customers' (future) needs and expectations well and too fragmented to change at the pace required.

Simplification was not a cosmetic exercise. It meant making hard choices: reducing duplication, letting go of local optimizations, and accepting that some autonomy had to be traded for coherence. It meant building shared platforms before they were popular and committing to them before outcomes were guaranteed. It also meant asking leaders (including myself) to change how we led, not just what we delivered. It meant reskilling the workforce or having to let them go.

The hardest part of transformation was not redesigning systems or improving the customer experience. It was unlearning habits that had once been rewarded.

This book has explored purpose, strategy, customer promise, branding, culture, behavior, leadership, and technology not as separate topics but as interdependent forces. You have seen how purpose provided direction when external expectations shifted and how culture determined whether strategy could survive contact with reality.

You have seen that empowerment without clarity creates anxiety, not ownership. That scale without simplicity produces distance, not efficiency. And that technology (whether digital platforms or AI) magnifies whatever intent already exists in an organization.

Perhaps most importantly, you have seen that transformation is not linear. Progress and resistance coexist. Momentum builds unevenly. And leadership requires staying present long after the excitement of a launch fades.

I shared my framework to help guide you through managing all relevant components for successful, flexible execution. It is for you to use but also alter to best suit you and your business's needs. If only to remember one thing: transformation succeeds only if the CEO connects all the dots with consistency of direction.

A DIRECT INVITATION TO YOU

I did not write this book to celebrate a transformation or to suggest it was flawless. I wrote it because I believe leaders deserve honest accounts of what change demands.

Transformation asks something of you personally. It tests your patience, your judgment, and your willingness to stand by decisions when their value is not immediately visible. It also forces you to confront your own assumptions about control, expertise, and identity.

My passion for this topic comes from having lived those tensions. From moments of doubt. From decision moments that felt lonely. From understanding that leadership is not validated by applause but by coherence over time.

If your organization is facing disruption, resist the urge to begin with technology alone. AI will accelerate whatever activities already exist. If those activities are unclear, fragmented, or misaligned, speed will not save you.

Begin instead with purpose. Be explicit about what you are willing to trade off—and what you are not. Stay close to your customers, not as an abstract idea but as a daily discipline. Explain your choices clearly, especially when they are unpopular. And accept that leadership today means being accountable not just for outcomes but for intent.

You will be judged. Often unfairly. Sometimes rightly. That is part of the role.

WHAT ENDURES BEYOND ANY SINGLE TRANSFORMATION

The world will continue to change faster than strategies can be perfected. Political priorities will reverse. Technologies will evolve. Societal expectations will shift again.

What endures is not certainty but direction.

Purpose, when lived rather than stated, becomes a stabilizing force. It allows leaders to adapt without drifting, to change course without losing credibility, and to act with conviction even when agreement is impossible.

Transformation is not about predicting the future correctly. It is about building organizations that can move, learn, and adjust without losing their integrity.

That is the work.

That is the responsibility and why leadership still matters. Especially now.

ACKNOWLEDGMENTS

Writing a book is one thing. Living one is far more demanding...and far more exciting. I wrote this book, with help, over the course of a year, on and off. But I lived this story for seven years as CEO of ING.

Who do you thank in a moment like this? The people who helped you write the book or the people who lived the journey with you?

First and foremost, I want to thank all my ING colleagues I worked with over my twenty-nine years at ING, who took this journey of disruption and transformation with me. You knew the future would demand change. You knew it would ask you to learn, unlearn, and evolve. And you chose to move forward together. If it had not been for you, we would never have been able to transform the bank so quickly after restructuring, nor to become the *Global Finance Best Bank in the World* and a reference point for transformation across our industry. That is an extraordinary achievement. What makes it even more meaningful is how it happened. You followed, you changed, and you challenged me, allowing us to deliver together. Without friction, there is no shine. I am deeply honored to have led you.

Thank you to the members of the Board who elected me and supported me until my final day in the role. Thank you to the members of my management team, who shared my vision and my passion but also challenged me, right until the end.

I could not have lived, nor written, this book without the support of my family. I needed them throughout my career but especially from the very first day I became CEO of ING. On October 2, 2013, my mother passed away unexpectedly, just as I was stepping into the role. As if the start had not brought enough challenges already. It was a period filled with mixed emotions, and I would not have made it through without the unconditional support of my family, my brothers, and my wider family. Having a large, warm family to fall back on makes all the difference.

My deepest thanks go to Patricia, my wonderful wife and steadfast partner, and to our children, Michelle and Maxim. They never complained, even when I could not give them the attention they deserved. Patricia, Michelle, and Maxim made it possible for me to lead ING through the remaining restructuring and transformation. Their love and support gave me the freedom to truly "do my thing."

I enjoy presenting. I enjoy inspiring people. I enjoy putting my thoughts on paper. Writing a book? For that, I needed help. Interestingly, the team that was there when I took over as CEO was also the team that helped me with this book from day one. Nanne, Peter, Hein, and Dorothy—thank you. Working together again felt like picking up a conversation we had only briefly paused. You helped me get the facts right, the storyline right, and just as importantly, put everything into perspective.

The same is true for the many people who were interviewed

for this book. It mattered to me that this was not only my version of the transformation but a collective reflection of how it was experienced. Your input was also important to get a better perspective on how you translated the purpose and strategy to your domains. This enriched the story and made it more insightful for readers and leaders of today. Thank you all for your openness and honesty.

My thanks as well to the beta readers who took the time, amid full professional lives, to read the manuscript before publication and offer constructive feedback. Your insights helped us see where the message resonated, where it needed tightening, and where greater clarity was required. You made this book stronger, more precise, and more useful for the leaders it is meant to serve.

And of course, my deepest professional thanks go to Lisa Caskey. When I first had the idea to write this book, I had no idea how to do it, or whether I could do it at all. Nanne introduced me to Scribe, and through them I met Lisa. From that moment on, Lisa carried this project with extraordinary dedication. She listened to me for days, asked thoughtful and sometimes uncomfortable questions, followed up when she heard different perspectives, and interviewed more than thirty people to ensure accuracy and balance.

We spent countless hours working together online. We also met in person: once for a full morning in Santa Monica, and again when Lisa came to Amsterdam for a long weekend to work with me and the team, to review and double-check the manuscript, and to truly experience the city and the country in which this story unfolded. Lisa, you are a remarkable professional. Your enthusiasm, your curiosity, your ability to reflect passion accurately on paper, and your genuine interest in understanding this journey made all the difference. And although ING no longer operates in US consumer banking, you became a true fan, exactly what every love brand hopes for.

Finally, my thanks to ING itself, and in particular to Steven, Marielle, and Raymond, for allowing me to write this book. Steven especially. People often expect tension between successors. I did not experience that, not with Jan, and not with Steven. Contexts change, and each leader must take the company forward in their own way. That is as it should be.

Marielle: If anyone truly knows ING, it is you. When documents seemed impossible to find, you found them. And Raymond…thank you for guarding the messaging throughout, always with ING's best interests at heart. All of you have orange blood running through your veins.

Like all ING people.

That is why this book is dedicated to them.

ABOUT THE AUTHOR

RALPH HAMERS is an internationally recognized banking leader known for transforming large incumbent institutions into purpose-driven, digital-first organizations. Over the course of his career as CEO of ING Group and later UBS Group, he has led some of the most ambitious restructurings, cultural transformations, and sustainability initiatives in global financial services. His leadership is defined by a belief that financial institutions are to be purpose led, must serve customers first, and embrace technology as a differentiator in experience, service, and advice.

Ralph served as chief executive officer of ING Group from 2013 to 2020, a period defined by profound strategic renewal following the global financial crisis. When he took over, ING was still completing its post-crisis restructuring. Under his leadership, the group continued the divestment of noncore businesses, including the IPO of NN Group and subsequent sales of NN Group and Voya Financial, as well as the sale of several insurance and asset management units across Asia. ING also exited or merged banking operations in markets such as India and

Thailand, simplifying the organization while strengthening its strategic focus. During this time, ING reduced its workforce from approximately 76,000 to 54,000 employees, reshaping the organization for long-term sustainability.

A major milestone of this restructuring was the final repayment under the €10 billion rescue facility from the Dutch State on November 7, 2014. Capital strength improved significantly, with the bank's CET1 ratio rising from below 11 percent to nearly 15 percent by the time Ralph stepped down as CEO.

Central to Ralph's leadership at ING was the articulation of a clear purpose: "Empowering people to stay a step ahead in life and in business." This purpose reframed ING's role in society by placing customer interests and broader social responsibility at the heart of decision-making. It was operationalized through the Orange Code, which defined shared values (being honest, prudent, and responsible) and behaviors that emphasized ownership, collaboration, and forward-thinking.

The Think Forward strategy put the customer at the core and made the customer experience the key differentiator. This focus on simplicity, clarity, and 24/7 digital accessibility drove accelerated customer growth, increasing ING's client base from 31.8 million to 39.3 million, with a large share served entirely through digital channels. ING proved that a digital/mobile bank could become a primary bank for its customers, growing the number of primary customers from 7.9M to 13.9M (10.6M are mobile-primary customers).

ING became the first global incumbent bank to adopt agile ways of working at scale, integrating technology, product, and business teams across retail and wholesale banking. This transformation turned ING into a global reference point for digital and organizational change, resulting in case studies by Harvard Business School, INSEAD, IMD, Delft University, BCG, and

McKinsey and attracting weekly visits from multinational companies seeking to learn from ING's experience.

Ralph also positioned ING as a leader in social responsibility and sustainability. He launched the Think Forward Initiative; an open-source global movement focused on improving financial health and financial decision-making in an increasingly digital world.

In climate and sustainability, ING was among the first banks to finance circular business models and to link loan pricing to ESG performance. Most notably, ING became the first global bank to set science-based targets for reducing the carbon footprint of its loan portfolio, formalized through the Terra Approach, with transparent annual reporting beginning in 2019. ING's leadership in this area led to top ESG ratings across major global indices and sustainability benchmarks.

ING was named *Best Bank in the World* in 2017 by *Global Finance*, and Ralph received numerous personal recognitions, including European Banker of the Year (2016), multiple top-ten rankings among global CEOs by the Reputation Institute (2018, 2019), and an Honorary Fellowship from London Business School (2019).

In 2020, Ralph became chief executive officer of UBS Group, where he led the firm through a period of strategic integration and strong performance. He developed and introduced UBS's purpose, "Reimagining the power of investing. Connecting people for a better world," and aligned the organization around a single integrated strategy spanning wealth management, investment banking, and asset management (One UBS).

At UBS, Ralph emphasized scale where it mattered, technological differentiation, organizational simplification, and cultural renewal. He oversaw the rollout of agile working across tens of thousands of employees, launched multiple digital wealth platforms, including UBS Key4, Circle One, and WE.UBS. Under his leadership, UBS delivered record financial results in 2021 and 2022 and nearly doubled its share price.

In 2023, Ralph played a central role in negotiating the rescue of Credit Suisse, helping stabilize the Swiss and global financial systems while protecting taxpayers and positioning UBS for long-term value creation.

NOTES

1   Transcript of the film used to introduce ING's new purpose, as part of the Think Forward strategy. It added context to the strategy and unveiled its purpose, shown before and after Ralph Hamers' "Power of Purpose" speech, during his global tour of ING offices in 2014. First shown during the weekend of March 29–30, 2014.

2   "ING Narrows Focus in 'Back to Basics' Shift," Investment & Pensions Europe, April 9, 2009, https://www.ipe.com/ing-narrows-focus-in-back-to-basics-shift/31422.article.

3   "ING to Integrate Its Local Insurance Brands in 'Back to Basics' Move," Reuters, July 2, 2009, https://www.emirates247.com/eb247/banking-finance/investment/ing-to-integrate-its-local-insurance-brands-in-back-to-basics-move-2009-07-02-1.27289.

4   In the beginning, ING had 76,000 employees, including the insurance company, but over time, the average number of employees ranged between 52,000 and 54,000.

5   This journey, and seeing how quickly things were changing, also convinced me of the need to do similar trips with the management board, which we did: Silicon Valley twice, Austin, New York, Hong Kong, Berlin, Tallinn. I also convinced Singularity University to start giving sessions in the Netherlands.

6   As part of ING's update to its investors in October 2016, we showed that our digital-primary customers interacted three times more often with us, purchased three times more products with ING, and generated a three times higher NPS.

7   This phase of ING's transformation has been extensively documented elsewhere. Detailed case studies have been developed by institutions such as Harvard, IMD, INSEAD, Delft University, BCG, and McKinsey, each examining different aspects of the journey. Rather than repeat that work here, readers interested in deeper analytical treatment can explore those materials directly through the institutions' published articles and case repositories.

8   René interviewed me when I exited ING, too.